P9-CJM-501

CAPTIVES OF SHANGHAI

THE STORY OF THE PRESIDENT HARRISON

In her pre-war look the SS *President Harrison* passes Treasure Island
outbound from San Francisco for the Orient. (American President Lines)

CAPTIVES OF SHANGHAI

The Story of the *President Harrison*

*David H. Grover
and Gretchen G. Grover*

*Western Maritime Press
Napa, California*

Copyright © 1989 David H. Grover and Gretchen G. Grover

All rights reserved. No part of the material protected by this copy-right notice may be reproduced or utilized in any form or by any means, electronic or mechanical, including photocopying, recording or by any informational storage and retrieval system without written permission from the copyright owner. Printed in the United States of America.

ISBN 0-9623935-0-9

Library of Congress Catalog Card Number: 89-051754

To the first of three generations of Naval Reservists in our family, Bertha Tilton Grover, YN 1/C, our mother and grandmother respectively, who served as a Yeomanette in World War I in the office of the Naval Overseas Transportation Service, this book is affectionately dedicated.

TABLE OF CONTENTS

ACKNOWLEDGEMENTS

The original idea for this book evolved from the confusion the senior author had once encountered over the 535s, 502s, and the ships bearing the names of presidents which were used as transports in World War II. This confusion complicated the task of writing the book on Army ships on which he was then working, but it also whetted his curiosity to know more about these ships and why they were so difficult to sort out correctly. When he learned that one of them had been captured by the Japanese and used as a military transport and yet nothing had been written about this ship--other than the standard paragraph in Captain Moore's book about the merchant ships lost in World War II--he gave serious thought to a book about the *President Harrison*.

Colette Carey, the archivist of the American President Lines (APL), suggested that the starting point on such a a book would be a visit to John Hallinan who had been a senior purser's clerk on the *Harrison* and who had since been a collector of key information about the ship. The next stop was at the home of Orel A. Pierson who had been master of the ship in 1941. Both these men live in the San Francisco Bay Area where the authors also live, so it was possible to talk to them early and often. After the initial contacts with these two key men it was clear that the adventures of the ship were indeed worthy of book-length treatment.

Since that time a number of people who were involved in the story have helped to pull it all together. Four of the surviving crewmembers who were particularly helpful are identified in the notes section of the book (relative to Chapter 8); these men are Howard Allred, Henry Behrens, Gilbert Monreal, and the previously mentioned Jack Hallinan. Others are listed in the bibliography among the dozens of people with whom interviews and/or correspondence were carried out. In some cases it was too late to talk to the eyewitness; surviving family members and friends have provided valuable insights.

Other individuals with both direct involvement in and strong recollections of the events in this book are the one-time Navy physician Dr. William T. Foley, the passenger agent Ed Wise, Captain Valdemar Nielsen of the *President Madison*, Colonel John A. White of the North China Marines, Captain Louis Duncan of the 4th Marines, and the late Henry F. Kay, the former APL representative in Shanghai who died while this book was being finished.

Interest in the project was high, and the response of those who were contacted was gratifying. This interest was a refreshing change from the indifference the senior author had encountered on an earlier venture into World War II maritime history.

Library research was carried out at the following California locations: California Maritime Academy at Vallejo; the National Maritime Museum at San Francisco; the National Archives at San Bruno; the University of California, Berkeley and Davis campuses; the Hoover Institution at Stanford University; the Naval Postgraduate School at Monterey; and the Napa Public Library.

Particularly helpful were two military history organizations: the Naval Historical Center and the U.S. Marine Corps Historical Center, both located at the Washington Navy Yard. Rear Admiral Kemp Tolley, USN (Ret.), assisted by calling our attention to the useful China Repository in the collection of the Naval Center and by supplying material from his own collection.

Translations of material from Japanese into English were provided by Akihisa Miyaji, and from Chinese into English by Douglas Liang.

Photographs for the book came from a wide variety of sources which are acknowledged individually on the credit line for each picture.

An Introduction
to the *President Harrison* Affair

In the fall of 1941 a voyage began routinely for the SS *President Harrison*, an American passenger liner departing San Francisco for the Far East. Passengers and crew were aware that their destination, although nominally still at peace, was a tense and unsettled part of the world. Nevertheless, they had no way of knowing that as they steamed toward the Orient they were soon to be part of the opening act of a strange drama of war and captivity then beginning in the Pacific, or the Pacific Theater, as ironically, it was soon to be called.

The *President Harrison* was never to know again the traditional completion of a ship's voyage: the ringing up of "Finished with Engines" on the engine order telegraph, and the beginning of a new set of pages in the logbook for the next voyage. Instead, after her heroic rescue of a Marine regiment from Shanghai she was destined to be captured by the Japanese while trying to rescue another detachment of U.S. Marines in North China from the threat of capture, then pressed into service as a Japanese troop ship, and subsequently sunk by an American submarine while transporting a load of Allied prisoners from Southeast Asia back to Japan.

Her crew was to spend three years and nine months--the entire period of American involvement in World War II--as prisoners of the Japanese, the first and largest group of merchant seamen to be so captured and the group that would spend as long in captivity as any other Americans during the war. Sixteen of her crew would not come back at all--some victims of the *Harrison*'s attempt to avoid capture, and others victims of the hardships of captivity.

Only fleeting references to the saga of the *President Harrison* and her crew appear in naval histories of World War II and in the virtually non-existent maritime histories of that war. Her capture a few hours after Pearl Harbor received only passing notice in the press. Even after the war, most of the limited recognition she received posthumously was as a Japanese ship and as a suspect in the disappearance of an anthropological treasure.

This account of the *President Harrison*'s final voyage attempts to counter the neglect of the ship by historians, and to provide some long-overdue awareness of and respect for the singular accomplishments of the ship and her crew. The story of the *President Harrison* is actually many stories. Primarily, of course, it is the story of a gallant ship and her equally gallant crew. But at times it also becomes the story of a sistership, a fleet of merchant ships, a steamship company, the American merchant marine in the twentieth century and government efforts to help that industry, two groups of Marines in China, the collapsing Asiatic Fleet of the U.S. Navy in 1941, the glittering city of Shanghai, and life in the prison camps of the Far East.

This study will explore the complex web of circumstances and ironies that surrounded the *Harrison* in her time of crisis, and how her final fate might have been quite different--had a few things not happened the way they did. There will be loose ends, of course, those things that do not fit neatly into the body of evidence that supports the conclusions of the study. There are even unsolved mysteries in the story of the *President Harrison*, not the least of which is the fate of the bones of Peking Man, scheduled to leave China on the last trip of the ship. An equally intriguing question is whether the *Harrison* was one of several unidentified ships reportedly sunk by American submarines along the China coast in 1942, only to be salvaged again to continue her infamous career as a Japanese troop ship until her documented demise in 1944. A third mystery concerns how much, or how little, the U.S. Navy knew about the existence and whereabouts of the *Harrison* as a Japanese ship, and whether her final sinking--like her initial capture--might have been prevented.

This, then, is the story of the *President Harrison*, a merchant ship thrust into an impossible mission by the Navy, the largest American ship to be captured in World War II, and a ship that was to give new meaning to the term *prisoner of war*.

ii

Chapter 1

The *President Harrison*:
Peacetime Years

To understand the circumstances which brought the SS *President Harrison* into such grave danger on the coast of China in 1941 it is helpful to know something of the 20-year history of the ship, as well as the maritime and military milieu in which she had operated.

The *President Harrison* was completed at the Camden, New Jersey, yard of the New York Shipbuilding Corporation in January of 1921. She was one of a class of seven ships generally known as the 502s, a designation based on their length between perpendiculars, a naval architect's term for the length measured from the stem of the ship to the back of the sternpost on which the rudder hangs. A similar class of ships built at the same time was designated as the 535s, but in this case the length used was the length overall. So, while the 502s seemed to be 33 feet shorter than the 535s, they were only about 12.5 feet shorter than their larger counterparts in terms of overall length.

Both classes of vessels, along with a third group known as Hog Island transports (for the Delaware River shipyard in which they were built), were designed and built under a program of the Emergency Fleet Corporation of the United States Shipping Board. The Shipping Board, dating from 1916 legislation, managed the construction and operation of the United States merchant fleet in World War I. The Emergency Fleet Corporation, a government corporation capitalized at $50 million, was responsible for building a number of types of merchant ships of all sizes and materials which were built in a number of shipyards on all coasts. The Shipping Board, together with the Merchant Fleet Corporation which later replaced the Emergency Fleet Corporation, was also to function as the controlling force in the operation of the American-flag merchant marine during the next decade and a half.

The 535s, 502s, and Hog Islanders were the three standard designs of the Emergency Fleet Corporation for combination passenger/cargo ships or transports. They were conceived as dual purpose ships that would spend at least part of their total service as military transports or hospital ships. All were built in East Coast yards. The construction of the sixteen 535s was divided among the Sparrow's Point yard of Bethlehem Steel, the Camden yard of New York Shipbuilding, and Newport News Shipbuilding. The seven 502s were all built at Camden, and the 12 Hog Islanders all came from the yard whose name they bore. Like all World War I shipbuilding programs, the transport program was conceived during the war, but the first ships were not even laid down until after the end of the war. Delays caused by frequent design changes pushed the completion dates for the 502s into late 1920 and early 1921.

The 502s were 522.5 feet in overall length, 62 feet in beam, and 41 feet in moulded depth. Loaded draft was about 32 feet. Their gross tonnage was 10,500, some 3,000 tons less than that of their 535 counterparts. They were powered by two triple expansion reciprocating steam engines and twin screws, with a total indicated horsepower of 7,000. Their operating speed was about 14.5 knots.

None of the Shipping Board transports was a thing of beauty. The Hog Islanders were built with a well-decked hull with no deck sheer, and their relatively short length produced a boxy appearance. Once described by the British naval architect J. H. Isherwood as "undeniably the ugliest of all passenger-carrying ships then operating in the North Atlantic," their origins at Hog Island were the source of some semantic embarrassment over their descriptive designation. The flush-decked 535s were no more handsome; they lacked sheer amidships where an ungainly hatch behind the bridge broke up the profile of the superstructure. With their peculiar double-ended look, Isherwood found that the 535s "did rather resemble the tin model liner, to be wound by a key inserted in the funnel." The 502s possessed much the same appearance as the 535s, except that they were well-decked ships and the gap in their superstructure to allow for the midship hatch was even larger than on the 535s. They were known collectively and affectionately as the "awkward squad."

Fortunately, for appearance sake as well as additional passenger capacity the superstructure of most of the 535s and 502s was closed up in conversion work done in the early 1930s, and these two classes then resembled more conventional passenger ships. This conversion work also increased revenues; originally the 502s had accommodations for 78 first class passengers, but with the new configuration the ships could carry many more. The *Harrison* in 1941 had space for 156.

The naming of the ships followed Shipping Board practices, and resulted in considerable confusion for years to come. Like most of the 535s, the 502s were all completed with names corresponding to state nicknames; the *President Harrison*, for example, was originally the *Wolverine State*. But the Shipping Board soon found that these nicknames were often little-known and thus unpopular. In April 1922, before many of the 535s and 502s were established in regular service, most of these ships were given the names of American presidents.

Unfortunately, there has been a great deal of confusion over the three classes of Shipping Board transports. In later years authoritative writers in the maritime field have carelessly referred to the "state" class or "president" class when, of course, there were two such classes. One writer even identified the 535s as Hog Islanders. Thus, from the beginning the Shipping Board transports had problems of identity. Even within a given name there could be some uncertainty, inasmuch as there had been two Presidents of the United States named Adams and two named Harrison; later there would be two Roosevelts and two Johnsons.

These problems were compounded by the steamship companies which operated the 535s and 502s, when they periodically reassigned presidential names among their ships. The rationale for this practice was not clear, although some names were apparently more prestigious than others and were reserved for use on newer ships. Later, the American President Lines, which operated "president"-named ships exclusively, became large enough that it was forced to develop contingency plans for use when the names were exhausted. These potential ship names included the names of 14 men who served as "President of the United States Assembled" before George Washington. Fortunately, these plans were never needed.

During Dollar Line days there were 30 names of ex-presidents available, and even without Washington and Arthur, names that were left unused for some reason, there seemed to be enough names to go around without the shuffling that went on. The *President Harrison* was fortunate, however; she was the only 502 that carried the same presidential name throughout her peacetime service, although no one seemed to know if she honored William Henry Harrison or Benjamin Harrison.

That service began on February 25, 1921, when she left San Francisco, still bearing the name *Wolverine State*, on her first voyage for the Pacific Mail Steamship Company on a route to the Orient and India. After her name change in 1922, she was taken out of the India service when that route was abandoned as uneconomical. She was then assigned briefly by the Shipping Board to a new service between the Pacific Coast and the East Coast of South America, a service which was sometimes known as the Pacific-Argentina-Brazil Line, for which Swayne & Hoyt Inc. was the general agent.

The United States Shipping Board had been given broader powers to operate ships than its successor agency, the United States Maritime Commission, was to possess after 1936. Among these powers, the Board could literally create a steamship company on paper, such as the Pacific-Argentina-Brazil Line, to provide service with Board-owned ships if no existing company wanted to serve the route. More than a dozen such companies were operated for the account of the Shipping Board by operating managers under contract with the Board.

The management-operating agreements known as MO-4s were generous to the operators, but caused the Shipping Board to lose an estimated $200 million in its first 18 months of operation. Under a typical agreement, a company or individual operating a government-owned ship was paid a 5% fee on the gross revenues of a voyage, with the Board underwriting all operating expenses. The arrangement tempted the operators to inflate both their revenues and expenses, leading the Seattle *Post-Intelligencer* to observe that the "M.O. is the most shameful piece of chicanery, inefficiency and looting of the public treasury that the human mind can devise."

The aim of the Shipping Board--to get American-flag vessels into service on a wide variety of routes--was attained for the moment, but the price, of course, was high. Like many of the runs, the West Coast to East Coast of South America service was unprofitable and likely to remain so. In late 1922 the *President Harrison* was temporarily taken out of this service; she was then loaned to the Los Angeles Steamship Company to replace the *City of Honolulu* which had burned at sea. She made four voyages in this role before returning to Swayne & Hoyt.

In mid 1923 the *Harrison* lost out on an opportunity to earn some national attention from the media. She had been assigned to carry President Warren G. Harding from San Francisco through the Panama Canal following his tour of the Pacific Coast and Alaska. However, Harding fell ill and died in San Francisco while the ship was undergoing alterations for the trip, and the chance for a moment in the limelight vanished for the *Harrison*.

Within a few months the gypsy years of drifting from one route and service to another ended when the ship was acquired by the Dollar Steamship Company. That organization which was soon to provide a new role for the 502s is worthy of more than passing note.

The Dollar Line was a rapidly-growing shipping conglomerate tracing its origins back 70 years through two separate lineages, one by blood and the other by corporate marriages. The corporate line of descent began with the Pacific Mail Steamship Company which first operated during California's gold rush days, bringing Argonauts and cargo from Panama to San Francisco; later it became the leading American company in the trans-Pacific trade. Once controlled by the Union Pacific Railroad and subsequently by the Southern Pacific system, Pacific Mail went through the corporate machinations of the robber baron era before it ultimately came under the control of the W. R. Grace steamship interests. In the 1920s, the Graces pulled out of the service to the Orient, placed their ships in intercoastal service, and sold the corporate shell of Pacific Mail to the Fleishacker banking interests in San Francisco who in turn sold it to the Dollar Company.

This latter company, a family holding company, was the true historical antecedent of the Dollar Steamship Company. Robert Dollar was one of the great Horatio Alger figures of his time, a man who rose from cook-shack boy in a lumber camp to the ranks of the lumber magnates. Starting late in life with a single steam schooner in 1895, he went on to own the largest fleet of steam schooners on the West Coast. Linking up with the Tacoma-based Pacific Steamship Company which had been forged together by H. F. Alexander from a number of small companies, the Dollar Line in the 1920s was emerging as a genuine steamship empire with both coastal and trans-Pacific service.

In September of 1923 the Dollar Line acquired from the Shipping Board not only the *President Harrison*, but all the other 502s as well. Five of these ships had been operated by U.S. Lines which, with the acquisition of a group of Hog Islanders coming off Army service, no longer needed them in the North Atlantic run. The other two, including the *Harrison*, had been under the control of Swayne & Hoyt, an operation for which the Shipping Board had no hope of success.

The price tag was about $3.8 million for all seven ships, none of it in cash. The *Harrison*'s share of the cost was $555,000, a price that reflected the glut of ships as a result of the wartime construction programs of the Emergency Fleet Corporation. The ship had cost $4,110,000 when completed two and a half years earlier, and was now being acquired in good condition at less than 14 cents on the dollar.

With the acquisition of these seven ships, the Dollar Line was destined to become a veritable shipping empire. Although the steamship business in the early twenties was scarcely profitable for American companies, the Dollar family believed that the time was ripe to launch a round-the-world service which would capitalize on the developing commerce between southeast Asia and Europe. The ungainly-looking 502s had been acquired primarily to serve this route.

The *President Harrison* now had the moment of glory she had been denied upon Harding's death when she was chosen to inaugurate the round-the-world service. On January 5, 1924, with bands playing for the assembled guests and spectators, the *Harrison*, after receiving a radio signal from President Coolidge in Washington, backed from her pier and began the first voyage in the soon-to-be-popular service that would make the Dollar Line a household word in America.

The schedule was to take the company's ships to Honolulu, Kobe, Shanghai, Hong Kong, Manila, Singapore, Penang, Col-

The *President Harrison* looked like this as she launched the round-the-world service of the Dollar Line in 1924. (Robert Dollar)

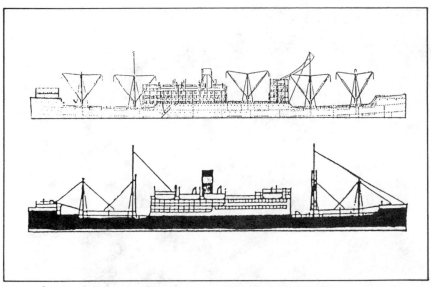

This comparative diagram shows how the appearance of the 502s was changed by closing up the hatch abaft the bridge.

Following her conversion, the *Harrison* was a much more handsome ship. (Allen Knight Maritime Museum)

Captain Orel A. Pierson commanded the *President Harrison* on her fateful voyage number 55. (American President Lines)

umbo, Suez, Port Said, Alexandria, Naples, Genoa, Marseilles, Boston, New York, Havana, Cristobal, Balboa and Los Angeles before returning to San Francisco. Variations in the schedule occurred from time to time, but generally 106 to 112 days were required for each voyage. Round-the-world fares to visit these romantic and near-legendary ports ran about $1,100 during the 1920s, and dipped as low as about $600 in the 1930s.

The concept initially proved highly profitable, and the Dollar Line enjoyed a number of years of success before the world-wide depression of the 1930s made the operation of virtually any ship a losing proposition. But, even more important, the 502s of the Dollar Line did an outstanding job of "showing the flag" on one of the most important maritime trade routes of the world during two decades of overcapacity and hard times in the shipping industry.

For the most part, serving that trade route was as uneventful for the 502s as it was successful. The *President Harrison* provided one minor exception, however, when in November 1926, she grounded near Shanghai. Accounts initially differed as to the location. The casualty notices in a weekly West Coast shipping magazine indicated that the site was within the Yangtze River, but later accounts correctly identified Bonham Island as the location, a rocky island off the coast south of the Yangtze delta on a dangerous short cut to and from the lightship. The *Harrison* was subsequently refloated and taken into Shanghai for repairs which took her out of service for about ten weeks. Ironically, 15 years later she would be put aground again off the approaches to the Yangtze, but that is getting ahead of our story.

After the success of the round-the-world service the Dollar Line became even more aggressive and expansionist. Despite the market crash of 1929 and ensuing depression, it ordered two large new liners, the *President Hoover* and *President Coolidge*, and bought two large old liners, vintage 1904, which it named the *President Johnson* and the *President Fillmore*. Its Puget Sound affiliate, American Mail Line, also bought several of the 535s from the Shipping Board. The Dollar family even tried unsuccessfully at this time to acquire the U.S. Lines.

But the passengers and cargoes to sustain this growth were not forthcoming, and in the 1930s the company began to lose growing amounts of money each year. A number of factors accelerated these losses, including the 1936 maritime strike on the West Coast, the 1937 grounding and loss of the *President Hoover* which was generating about one quarter of the line's revenue, and the freewheeling management style of the Dollar family. But it was the heavy debt load acquired in expanding that eventually brought the company to the edge of bankruptcy. Finally the once-prosperous steamship line could go no further; in 1938 the company was surrendered to the U.S. Maritime Commission in return for being released from all liabilities.

As a result, the United States government actually owned a real West Coast steamship company, not just a paper line consisting of a route. As the holder of almost 90% of the company's stock the Maritime Commission named former California Senator William G. McAdoo to be Chairman of the Board. McAdoo, a national power in Democratic Party politics, had been Secretary of the Treasury, Chairman of the Federal Reserve Board, and wartime czar of railroads and coastwise shipping in the administration of his father-in-law, Woodrow Wilson. The new management renamed the company; it now became American President Lines, Ltd. On the house flag and on the blue stacks of the company's ships a stylized white eagle on a red background replaced the familiar white dollar sign on a red band and blue background.

After a lay-up during the corporate changeover the *President Harrison* and her sister ship 502s went back to sea. Soon the plodding tempo of the depression years began to give way to the stepped-up beat of rearmament. When the war in Europe began in 1939 ships were once again in demand. A number of the 535s which had been laid up were acquired in 1940 and 1941 by the Army and the Navy; four more were sold abroad. The seven Hog Islanders were used in the North Atlantic trade by the U.S. Lines were transferred to the Belgian flag in 1940 in a joint-venture agreement which circumvented the restrictions of the neutrality laws on American ships trading in Europe. Ironically, two of the 535s and six of the Hog Islanders transferred to foreign registry were sunk or otherwise lost by mid-1941, whereas all the 502s were still steaming along at 14.5 knots for the American President Lines.

Although the *Harrison* and the other round-the-world liners had been displaying a large American flag on the hull to indicate

8

the status of a neutral, the war in Europe had made the trips though the Mediterranean too risky. German troops had overrun Greece and Crete to the north, while German and Italian forces were driving eastward across North Africa toward Egypt. With the Mediterranean thus ringed by Axis forces, American President Lines in mid-1940 found it necessary to re-route most of the round-the-world 502s around the Cape of Good Hope rather than along the southern edge of Europe.

The summer of 1941 marked an even greater change in the operation of the *President Harrison*. After 17 years in the round-the-world trade she was put instead into trans-Pacific service. Only one ship, the *President Buchanan*, remained in limited round-the-world service. During July that ship received minor damage in an air raid at Suez.

During that same month, after learning of Japanese intentions of moving south into Indochina to threaten Singapore, President Roosevelt froze all Japanese assets in the United States and established a trade embargo. Japan's response was to rationalize further her need for military action insuring her access to critical raw materials from southeast Asia, particularly oil. After occupying Indochina that summer in defiance of the United States, Japan made war inevitable, and public opinion in the island nation accepted that inevitability.

While Americans may not have felt that war was unavoidable, they had at least given some thought to the possibility. Public attitudes toward Japan changed markedly during the pre-war years, reflecting a swing from isolationism to intervention. In 1938, only a few weeks after the sinking of the American Navy gunboat *Panay* in the Yangtze River by the Japanese, 70% of American voters favored withdrawal of all Americans from China; even on the West Coast such feelings were held by about two-thirds of those with opinions. But a year and a half later, after Congress repudiated the commercial treaty of 1911 with Japan, 82% of American voters favored an embargo on war materials. By 1940 the percentage approving the embargo had risen to 96%. In 1941 Americans were asked if they would be willing to risk war "to keep Japan from becoming more powerful." The *yes* vote reached 51% in July and 70% in September before dipping to 64% in November. However, it is probably fair to say that few Americans at that time had any concept of Japan's ability to make war.

The year 1941 had marked the beginning of the third decade of service for the *Harrison* and her sister ships. Alone among the Shipping Board passenger/cargo ships, the 502s had all remained fully employed as American-flag merchant ships during their entire careers, most of which had been spent under the house flags of the Dollar line and the American President Lines. A construction program was underway to replace these reliable vessels with new Maritime Commission C3P passenger type hulls, but only a few such ships had been completed and some of these were being grabbed up by the Army and Navy.

The record achieved by the 502s was an enviable one. For two decades they had earned a fine reputation as dependable hard-working ships. In spite of their reciprocating engines and homely looks, they were universally regarded as good "sea boats," a term used by mariners to denote a ship which could handle rough weather with a minimum of discomfort to those on board and damage to the cargo. They were also respected as efficient ships which could maintain tight schedules through quick turnarounds. Sailing westward from San Francisco every two weeks for over 17 years these ships had amassed in excess of 10 million miles on more than 350 trips around the world. As the first of the breed and the one whose name had been unaltered by the whims of time, the *Harrison* personified this remarkable achievement.

Even though she would never go around the world again, the *Harrison* remained in service as a passenger liner in the fall of 1941, still never having served as the troop ship she was originally designed to be. That status, however, was soon to change.

Chapter 2

Underway to the Unknown

In August of 1941 the *President Harrison* made her first trans-Pacific round trip since the early 1920s. The passenger list was swelled by a number of Army personnel, largely national guardsmen, going out to the Philippines, but she remained a civilian liner, one of the last such ships operating under the American flag. By this time virtually all other passenger ships, except for a few in Caribbean and coastal service, had already been requisitioned for military service. Why the American President Lines was allowed to keep the 502s in service is not clear, but this situation may have reflected the special status the company was beginning to display as an instrument of American foreign and military policy.

Arriving back in San Francisco on October 10th with a strategic cargo of rubber, the *Harrison* had a week to discharge and to prepare for her next trip to the Orient. Voyage number 55 was the designation in the logbook and in official records for the upcoming round trip. There would never be a voyage 56 for the ship.

Shipping articles for the voyage were signed on board on October 15, 1941. The articles are a traditional yet official agreement between the master and crew concerning the nature of employment, wages, length and duration of the voyage, and other contractual terms. On this document voyage 55 was described as a "voyage from the port of San Francisco, California, to Manila, P. I., and such other ports and places in any part of the world as the Master may direct, and back to a final Pacific Coast port of discharge in the United States to be designated by the Master."

While the description of the voyage may have seemed somewhat nebulous for a liner which had booked cargo and passengers for several other ports, it was by no means as indefinite as the terminology that was soon to be used on merchant ships after the outbreak of war when it would read "to a point in the Pacific Ocean west of San Francisco, California, and from that point to such other ports and places in any part of the world as the Master may direct..."

In addition to destination, the articles deal with a number of features of employment. Even the daily minimum ration of foodstuffs is specified. The articles are an outgrowth of the days when sailors were impressed into involuntary service. The document is a contract providing for an offer and a voluntary acceptance of a minimum level of pay, provisions, and treatment. In the *Harrison's* time the signing of articles on an ocean-going voyage was a ceremony of sorts, witnessed by a Shipping Commissioner (in 1941 a relatively new function for the U.S. Coast Guard), who assured that each seaman's decision to make the voyage was indeed voluntary.

Although the document served as an employment contract, the shipping articles may have protected the seamen to a greater degree than the employer. Breaking the agreement through desertion was an offense under maritime law, but the penalty was only forfeiture of effects and wages left aboard. Furthermore, inasmuch as a seamen was entitled to draw up to one half his earned wages upon arriving in port and was entitled to repatriation from a foreign port through the United States consul, the existence of a contract provided little deterrence to a seaman who was tempted to desert a vessel in a foreign port-- at least in peacetime.

In 1941 it was becoming increasingly difficult to get good crews for merchant vessels. The stepped up activity of national defense was creating a broad employment market which siphoned off some of the trained manpower of a merchant marine which had already shrunk in size through years of depression. A round-the-world liner such as the *Harrison* had a particularly difficult personnel problem in that she touched at East Coast as well as West Coast ports, thus providing an opportunity for seamen to leave the vessel early without breaking articles, even though the voyage might not be officially complete. Furthermore, the numerous ports of call overseas provided additional places for seamen to leave the ship lawfully for medical reasons, or unlawfully for reasons of their own. The result was a certain degree of turnover, in spite of the fact that the crew was under the contractual provisions of the articles. Even on voyage 55 of the *Harrison* such turnover existed, making it difficult to determine exactly who was on board during the impending adventure which was to terminate the voyage.

Under maritime law all persons employed aboard a vessel other than the master are regarded as seamen, regardless of the individual billet or capacity in which they serve. Accordingly, the 165 people who signed on the *President Harrison* were all seamen even though only a few had a job title which included that term. In this sense, the merchant seamen of the *Harrison* included: mates, radio operators, night watchmen, a carpenter, a bos'n, quartermasters, able bodied seamen, ordinary seamen, pursers, clerks, a surgeon, engineers, junior engineers, oilers, a deck engineer, a plumber, an electrician, reefer engineers, a maintenance man, water tenders, firemen, storekeepers, wipers, supervisory stewards, a stewardess, cooks, bakers, butchers, pantrymen, scullions, a printer, a yeoman, a painter, a bartender, a linen steward, deck stewards, a smoking room steward, waiters, room stewards, bathroom stewards, porters, janitors, messmen, bell boys, and laundrymen. Basic monthly salaries for these positions ranged from $62.50 to $362.25.

When encountering the term merchant seamen in wartime histories it is easy for the reader to visualize an archtypical sturdy breed of weathered men with crows-footed eyes and wearing watch caps. In reality, the seamen of a passenger ship collectively did all sorts of jobs requiring a wide variety of skills, strength and apparel.

Because the crew of the *Harrison* would later be called upon to spend longer in captivity than virtually any other Americans in World War II, it may be useful in understanding that ordeal to know more about this group. As with the stereotyped image of merchant seamen, the typical image of the prisoner of war may not accurately fit these people.

By conventional standards the crew that signed on the *President Harrison* for voyage 55 was a rather diverse group. But that diversity appeared much greater by some standards than by others. For example, when compared to the crews of the few naval vessels that were soon to be captured early in the upcoming war, the *Harrison*'s personnel were indeed a "motley crew." On naval vessels the crew was young, with the oldest men-- generally the captain and a few of the chief petty officers--no more than 40. The homogenous Navy crew could be expected to be in excellent health; it was made up largely of native-born

American citizens and some Filipinos, the turnover was slow and controlled, and it had an internal back-up system of command and discipline. By contrast, the *Harrison* crew, as we shall see shortly, was a heterogenous mix of ages, races, states of health, and length of service aboard; further, no back-up system of discipline was in place. These differences would later become significant when each group faced the rigors of captivity.

But viewed by the standards of practice within the West Coast maritime industry at that time, there was nothing particularly unique about the crew of the *Harrison*. The Dollar Line and the American President Lines had always used racially diverse crews, as mixed as the law would permit. For decades the Dollar Line had employed foreign seamen to reduce labor costs as much as possible; some of its ships were even registered in Great Britain, Canada, and China. The LaFollette Seamen's Act of 1915, pushed by the West Coast maritime leader Andrew Furuseth, had required that a large proportion of the crews of American-flag vessels be able to understand English. When Dollar and other West Coast steamship operators in apparent violation of that legislation increased the use of Chinese in deck gangs in the 1920s, the Shipping Board intervened with a ruling that no Orientals could serve either on deck or in the engine room. It also decreed that Filipinos be excluded from these departments, but later rescinded that order.

In 1928 the Jones-White Act provided that half the crews of American-flag vessels with mail contracts could be aliens during the first four years of the contract, which was welcome news to the cost-conscious Dollar management. During the late 1920s and early 1930s more than half the crews of the various Dollar-affiliated steamship lines were Chinese nationals. As late as 1930 the Dollar Line itself employed on its ships 2,048 Chinese nationals out of a total of 5,427 employees afloat, or 38% of the total.

However, the final word on crewing came in the Merchant Marine Act of 1936. That legislation required that 90% of the unlicensed crew of subsidized passenger ships be citizens, and it was under this law that the *Harrison* was crewed in 1941. Thus, viewed in terms of the historical patterns of crewing within the company's vessels, the *President Harrison*'s crew in 1941 did not reflect the extreme ethnic diversity that had once characterized earlier crews.

For voyage number 55 among the 165 people on the original crew list were 14 Orientals, 3 Filipinos, 19 Blacks, and 6 Latinos. Foreign-born members of the crew totalled 45, 32 of whom were fully naturalized and 13 of whom were in various stages of the process of becoming citizens. The largest group, of six, was from Germany, with five each from England and China, four each from Ireland and the Philippines, three from Hungary, two each from Brazil, Russia and Switzerland, and one each from Norway, Denmark, Sweden, Austria, Canada, San Salvador, Poland, Scotland, Mexico, Turkey, Australia, and France.

Reduced as it might have been over that of earlier ships, the ethnic diversity of the crew of the *Harrison* was still great enough to confuse the Japanese when the ship was captured. Americans were as stereotyped by the Japanese as the Japanese were by Americans. As a result, when the Japanese found a number of Orientals and Blacks on the ship, as well as a number of Caucasians speaking with European accents, it was difficult for them to know how to classify these prisoners for purposes of internment.

In one other respect, however, diversity was virtually non - existent on the *Harrison*; the crew was almost completely male. The lone woman was 55-year-old Mrs. Clara Main, a native of Scotland, who was a stewardess. She, too, would become an administrative problem for her captors.

But it was in the matter of age that the crew of the *Harrison* differed the most, both within its own ranks and with respect to comparable Navy crews. At the time they signed aboard, the members of the crew ranged from 18 to 66 years. The median age of the crew was 38 which would correspond roughly to the *highest* age on a Navy ship of similar size crew. Four of the crew were in their late teens, 48 were in their twenties, 38 in their thirties, 43 in their forties, 26 in their fifties, and 5 in their sixties.

Merchant seamen at that time, even though mature in years, were often relatively rootless people. Only 35 men listed wives as next of kin on the crew list; 10 men reported no address and no next of kin. No more than half the crew listed addresses in western states or Hawaii, so it was not necessarily a "West Coast" crew in the ordinary sense.

As a company with a union contract American President Lines was obliged to hire its crews through the hiring halls of the various maritime unions. Among licensed officers the mates came from the Masters, Mates, and Pilots, while the engineers came from the Marine Engineers Beneficial Association, and the radio officers from the American Communications Association. The unlicensed deck personnel were members of the Sailors' Union of the Pacific, the engine department personnel from the Marine Firemen, Oilers, Watertenders and Wipers union, and the steward's department personnel from the Marine Cooks and Stewards union.

The man who, in the quaint wording of the shipping articles, would "go for master" and command this crew on voyage 55 was Orel A. Pierson. Forty-one years old and a veteran master with APL and the Dollar Line before that, Pierson was relatively new aboard the *Harrison* but had served in most of the 502s and 535s operated by the two companies.

Born in Massachusetts in 1900 but growing up in the family home in Rockland, Maine, where his ancestors had been seafaring people for more than a century, Pierson had first gone to sea during the summer at age 15. His first ship was the three-masted schooner *Frank Huckins*, owned by an uncle. When he eventually went to sea full time he sailed on deck as an unlicensed seaman in intercoastal vessels.

Even after he acquired a mate's license at age 19, he continued to sail as a quartermaster and able seaman because of the depressed maritime labor market of the early 1920s. Moving to the United States Lines, he sailed on the North Atlantic for several years, during which he acquired his first position as a ship's officer. When the *President Polk* in which he was serving burned and was laid up for repairs in 1924, Pierson was allowed to stay on while most of the crew was laid off, even though he was a very junior officer.

Even before her fire and reconditioning, the *Polk* was part of the five ship deal which sent the 502s of the U.S. Lines to the Dollar Line. Subsequently, Orel Pierson made the trip through the Panama Canal to deliver the ship, and his long career as a West Coast mariner with Dollar and APL began. After working his way up through second and chief mate billets, he eventually received his first command, the *President Hayes*. He also met and married a San Francisco girl, and put down permanent roots in the San Francisco Bay Area.

Although he was in no sense only a relief captain, Pierson

16

through the years did carry out a number of vacation relief stints for various company skippers, thus acquiring broad experience on many of the ships of the Dollar and APL fleet, although he never served in the *Harrison* during this time. In 1941 he had been serving as the permanent master of the *President Taft*, a 535, when that ship was requisitioned by the Army for service as a transport. Even though he was particularly fond of that ship, he had to give her up and take on a new assignment.

As his next command the company planned to give Captain Pierson the new *President Polk*, a C3P passenger/cargo ship then under construction at Newport News, Virginia. But the new ship would not be ready until the fall of 1941, so he agreed to a temporary assignment as master of the *President Harrison* on her first trans-Pacific voyage in August. The regular skipper of the *Harrison*, Duncan Ward, had decided to take a job ashore with the Cramp shipyard in Philadelphia, leaving the master's position open. As a senior captain, Pierson had earned the right to command the *Polk* as a more prestigious new passenger ship, so a clear understanding existed that the *Harrison* was a one-trip assignment for him. The one trip stretched to two, however, when Captain Pierson returned from voyage 54 in October to learn that the *Polk* was still not ready, and that the company needed him for one more trip in the *Harrison*.

Thus, Orel Pierson's presence as master of the *President Harrison* on voyage 55 resulted from a combination of several relatively minor happenings and decisions. If any of these factors had been different, he might not have been there. But that is the way that fate operates, is it not? Similar "if only"s may have existed for all aboard the ship.

Sailing day, October 17th, arrived in San Francisco. It had been hot on the California coast as it often is in October, but a fresh breeze had brought cooler air and some cloudiness to the Bay Area.

On that day the San Francisco *Examiner* took more than casual notice of the fact that the cabinet of Prince Fuminaro Konoye had fallen in Tokyo on the previous day. In solid, one-inch block headlines it proclaimed, "U.S. JAP CRISIS GROWS." In sub-heads it announced, "Tokio Cabinet Falls, War Regime Looms."

Konoye was the last prime minister to make any effort to avoid war with the United States. Negotiations were to continue, even after his departure from the political scene, but they were destined to go nowhere. The American position was firm; Japan must get out of China. The Japanese negotiating posture was now to become a sham as plans for the Pearl Harbor attack, originally drawn up in September, reached the implementation stage. With Konoye's resignation the Emperor was quick to broaden the powers of his next choice for the position, giving him three portfolios as prime minister, war minister, and home minister. That choice, announced the next day, was a man soon to be hated and caricatured in the United States perhaps even more than Hitler: General Hideki Tojo.

The *Examiner* routinely carried a lot of shipping news, but for some reason the departure of the *President Harrison* went unreported. Ironically, there was considerable attention devoted to the upcoming joint meeting of the American Merchant Marine Conference and the Propeller Club beginning that weekend in San Francisco, and an editorial inveighed against the arming of merchant ships as a sure way to drag the United States into war. But, other than the notice that mails were closing at nine in the morning for the Philippines, there was no indication that any ship was sailing for the Far East.

In New York for that date the *Journal of Commerce* carried the sailing notice for the ship, but listed no destination for the voyage even though most sailing notices still contained that information for other ships. A shroud of mystery was beginning to fall over the *Harrison*.

The secrecy was particularly awkward for the passengers. Most were military men going to Manila; others were going back to posts in business or missions in the Far East after periods of leave in the States. For both groups, sailing for Manila or Shanghai on a ship whose departure was not publicly acknowledged must have been a bit unnerving.

For weeks the sailing schedules of American ships had become increasingly secretive. In June of 1941 the U.S. Post Office had ceased using the names of vessels and sailing dates in announcing the closing times for mail to general areas of the world. The sailing cards for West Coast steamship companies published in shipping journals often now substituted "a vessel" for the names of individual ships, and early, mid and late-month departures for specific dates. The American President Lines still proclaimed its round-the-world service, but most of the service consisted of the flow of new "president" liners, the C3Ps, from the shipyards of the East Coast to the West Coast and on to the Pacific under military charters or agreements with the Maritime Commission. The *President Madison*, the last ship which would make the total round-the-world voyage, albeit more by accident of fate than by intent, had left San Francisco two weeks earlier. The *Harrison* would see her briefly in Shanghai in six weeks before each ship went on her separate and dangerous way.

But for the present on Friday afternoon, October 17, 1941, no bands were playing for the *President Harrison* as they had done on that illustrious day 17 years earlier when she had started on the first round-the-world voyage for the old Dollar Line. Now she made a quiet departure without fanfare from her berth at the APL terminal at pier 42, furtively passed under the Bay Bridge and the Golden Gate Bridge, and soon took her departure from the lightship as her official--and final--farewell to San Francisco and the continental United States.

Although the West Coast may have been more concerned about events in the Far East than most of the rest of the United States, the mood of the people there was still relatively calm. Those aboard the *Harrison* may have had greater worries than those Californians from whose midst they had just departed, but as land faded from view so did many of the concerns. As any seafarer can testify, it is difficult to think about global issues aboard a ship sailing peacefully across broad expanses of ocean. Although the *President Harrison* had shortwave radios on board and thus was in general touch with the world situation, there was no more of a sense of impending international crisis aboard the ship than there was among the general population of the United States.

Five days later the arrival of the *Harrison* in Honolulu, although no secret there, again went unreported in the shipping news of the *Examiner*. By this time Hawaii was on virtually a war footing compared to the West Coast, and the first impact of the tense situation in the Far East was felt on the ship. Beyond Hawaii the Navy had begun to exercise control of merchant shipping. Now the naval authorities decided to send the *Harrison* on to the Orient via a roundabout southerly route rather than by a direct route that would have taken the ship close to the Carolines and Marianas, island territories administered by Japan under mandates of the old League of Nations.

This decision reflected two realities. First, the Navy, which wanted all shipping to the Philippines to go under convoy, had no convoy making up at that time which was soon to sail. Use of a safer, more southerly route would permit the *Harrison* to sail immediately, albeit alone, for the Orient. The second consideration was a limited fresh water capacity on the *Harrison*. A long, direct trip, particularly to Manila, would tax that capacity, whereas a voyage made in island-hopping stages would not, since water could be obtained at intermediate ports.

The Navy's influence over the *Harrison* may also have been enhanced at this point by calling into play a special status enjoyed by the ship, a status whose effect no one really understood fully because it had never been exercised before, at least overtly.

The *Harrison* flew the flag of the Naval Reserve, signifying that she was a merchant vessel commanded by a Naval Reserve officer and that at least half of her eligible officers were also Naval Reservists. Captain Pierson had indeed been a lieutenant commander in the Naval Reserve since 1934. By his own admission made years later, he had engaged in courier and intelligence work for a number of years in the 1930s and early 1940s.

As described in Navy publications, ships flying the Naval Reserve flag "have been designated by the Secretary of the Navy as suitable for service as naval auxiliaries in time of war." No count seems to be available as to how many ships had this status in 1941, but a decade earlier 140 out of 1,150 American merchant ships were eligible to fly the flag.

What was not clear under this arrangement was how the status of a Naval Reserve ship differed from that of a non-reserve ship, particularly for ships of the same type that had been built by the government as transports. Many 535s and 502s were to serve as naval auxiliaries in World War II; some of these ships apparently had not been Naval Reserve vessels. Was the Naval Reserve status of a ship a meaningless designation in peacetime-- since all ships were subject to governmental requisition in wartime--or did it somehow translate into greater Navy control and use of a ship? While the answer may never be clear in the case of the *Harrison*, representing one of the numerous mysteries surrounding the ship, the Japanese who were later to capture her obviously felt that the connection to the U.S. Navy was

20

significant.

On October 24, 1941, just a week out of San Francisco, the *Harrison* left Honolulu on the next leg of her final voyage, again unreported in the shipping news of her home port. This time she was bound for Manila by way of Suva in the Fiji Islands. Suva was a major port at which ships regularly called for water, cargo, or provisions. It lay about 2,775 nautical miles southwest of Honolulu, about an eight day trip for a 502.

Each of the next several legs of the voyage would require careful selection of courses and accurate navigation to avoid the many islands and reefs of the South Pacific and the seas and archipelagos with exotic names: the Coral Sea, New Hebrides, Arafura Sea, the Mollucas, the Celebes Sea and the Sulu Sea. Although the trackline of the ship would coincide with standard steamship routes, this was a part of the world not intimately familiar to the crew of the *Harrison*, making a high degree of prudent seamanship absolutely essential.

Without the logbook of the ship as a reference it is difficult to reconstruct accurately the timetable of each leg of the voyage beyond Honolulu. On the passage to Suva the ship crossed the Equator, normally the scene of shellback initiations for those crewmembers and passengers who had not previously ventured into the southern hemisphere. This crossing occurred near Howland Island where Amelia Earhart had disappeared on her 1937 flight.

On October 28th the *Harrison* crossed the International Date Line, a meridian which had double meaning for the crew. First, it marked the point where a date on the calendar was lost while crossing westbound (normally to be regained on a return eastbound trip, but lost to round-the-world ships which gained it back an hour at a time for months to come while changing time zones). Second, and more important to the crew, the 180th meridian marked the beginning of their war zone bonuses.

The war zone bonuses were part of a rider to the shipping articles, negotiated between American President Lines and the unions representing the officers and crew. This rider provided for a bonus of 2/3 of base pay to be paid each crew member for each day spent west of the 180th meridian. The arrangement was a specific acknowledgement that there were hazards to be encountered by merchant seamen on ships that entered any of five specified war zones, one of which was the Far East.

Unfortunately for everyone, there were certain ambiguities in the agreement, requiring a court case after the war before the crew members were able to collect the full amount of their bonuses.

The *President Harrison* reached Suva a few days after crossing the Date Line, which would have made the date around the first of November. After replenishing her water supply the ship departed for Manila, still some 4,781 miles away via the route projected by the captain--only 88 miles less than the direct Honolulu to Manila distance would have been.

Enroute, the ship touched at two other way ports, Port Moresby in Papua where a pilot was taken for passage through the Torres Strait, and at Darwin on the north coast of Australia. By the time she reached Darwin the ship had logged 2,947 miles from Suva, with the date now about November 11th. Manila still lay 1,834 miles to the north.

The long, but thus far uneventful, trip was resumed once again. One month and 9,648 miles after she had left San Francisco, the *Harrison* on November 17th finally steamed through the minefields surrounding Corregidor, and entered the broad expanse of Manila Bay.

Chapter 3

The Expedition to Shanghai

While the *Harrison* had been enroute from Honolulu to Manila, the long way, via Suva, Port Moresby, and Darwin, much had been happening during that month that would influence the future course of events for the ship. At the end of October the *President Taylor*, another 502 of the American President Lines on a schedule about four weeks ahead of the *Harrison*, had been directed by the Navy to cancel a scheduled stop at Shanghai to go to Manila instead. At that time the port of Shanghai was ordered closed to all American vessels until further notice. The American President Lines had already closed its passenger office there, but still maintained a general office. With the *Harrison* having both passengers and cargo for the Chinese port, all those aboard the ship were curious as to what the Navy would do when it was time for her to sail.

Preparations for war had moved ahead on both sides. During the first week in November, Japanese naval commanders received Admiral Yamamoto's Order Number One, the final operational order for the Pearl Harbor attack on December 8, 1941, Far East time. The War Council, Cabinet, and Emperor all approved the document.

American military leaders in the Philippines knew the war was coming; they could only guess at the timing and the details. As the capital city of what had been an American trusteeship, Manila in the fall of 1941 was a city waiting for war. It had known the presence of the American Army and Navy for decades, but it had never encountered the kind of military build-up it was now experiencing. Inasmuch as the *Harrison*, for all practical purposes, was now to become a ship of the U.S. Navy, it is essential to know something of the military situation and thinking which prevailed in this strategic city.

The updated Rainbow 5 War Plan of the United States assumed that the Philippines would be a target of Japanese military action in a coming war, and that the large American garrison there would fight a defensive action for six months until the Pacific Fleet could battle its way westward with the materiel and personnel to defeat the Japanese. This plan, incorporating long-standing assumptions about the initial indefensibility of the Philippines, had been modified somewhat by a new optimism generated by General Douglas MacArthur whose views on the Philippines were widely respected. During the previous decade MacArthur had been successively Chief of Staff of the United States Army, military advisor to the Philippines, Field Marshal of the Philippine Army, and now Commander, U.S. Army Forces, Far East. The general believed that an attack would not be mounted against the Philippines until April of 1942. He was confident that the American and Philippine armies, augmented by reinforcements and supplies then in the procurement pipeline, could repel the Japanese. This effort would be aided immeasurably by new bombers which were on the way, B-17s which had demonstrated their effectiveness on a lend-lease basis for the Royal Air Force over Germany.

MacArthur's Navy counterpart was Admiral Thomas C. Hart, USN, Commander, Asiatic Fleet. Hart had been inherently pessimistic about the chances of defending any portion of the Far East. With the blessing of the Chief of Naval Operations he had pulled his headquarters out of Shanghai in late 1940, over the protest of the State Department which thought that such a move could be construed as a retreat, further encouraging Japanese agression.

At his new headquarters in Manila in the fall of 1941 Admiral Hart now felt that perhaps MacArthur's assessment was correct. As a result he had slowed the relocation of his forces to the south where a joint British-Dutch-American fleet was to come into being in time of war to defend Southeast Asia. He had even tried to convince the Navy Department that basing his fleet in Manila would make more sense than commiting his ships to a poorly-planned joint Allied fleet that existed largely on paper.

However, on November 20th he was overruled by Secretary of the Navy Frank Knox, and ordered to send the bulk of his fleet south. The Asiatic Fleet was considerably smaller than the Pacific Fleet, but the force that left Manila shortly thereafter was, nevertheless, potentially an effective striking force consisting of two cruisers, eight destroyers, and a tender. Unfortunately, it was dispersed over an enormous area, thus reducing its ability to impact significantly on future engagements.

Hart's other major concern was the safety of several ships and units still in China. These included five river gunboats, four of which were in the Yangtze River, and two detachments of U.S. Marines: the 4th Regiment in the International Settlement in Shanghai, and a group of embassy and legation guards in North China.

For some time Hart had been seeking authorization to remove these forces from China because their position was so utterly untenable in the face of imminent outbreak of hostilities. He was so pessimistic about the fate of the 4th Marines that he took it upon himself to hold back replacements destined for those units, assigning such men instead to other units at Cavite. He was quoted as saying that if by chance he was unable to get the Marines out of China, he "could at least stop sending any more Marines there until someone bawled us out most vociferously. They never did."

Early in September he concurred with his two commanders in Shanghai, Colonel Samuel L. Howard of the 4th Marines and Rear Admiral William A. Glassford of the Yangtze River Patrol, when they joined with the American Consul General, Frank P. Lockhart, in recommending the evacuation of all naval forces from China.

Hart forwarded his concurrence to the Navy Department with the recommendation that the evacuation of the Marines in Shanghai and in North China be effected by the USS *Henderson*, the venerable Navy transport which was due to visit the Far East in late September on a regular personnel rotation run.

This request was denied, but Hart was told that the Navy and State Departments were to hold conferences within a few weeks to consider the problems of such a withdrawal of American forces and the possible effect of ongoing negotiations with the Japanese to avoid the impending conflict. Hart protested to no avail that the question could not be put off even a few weeks. In the meantime, the *Henderson* had come--at least to Chinwangtao in North China--and gone, and the Marines were still in China.

Finally, on November 10, 1941, several days after the Shanghai press had reported the news, the official authorization came from Washington to bring the gunboats and Marines out of China. Admiral Hart ordered the Navy vessels to make plans for a quick departure for Manila, an ocean voyage for which the river gunboats had not been designed. The Marines were ordered to load their gear and otherwise be ready for evacuation. Now the problem facing Hart's staff became one of implementation; *how* would the evacuation take place? The 750 Marines in Shanghai became the first priority.

The port of Manila was full of American ships, most of which were freighters under the operational control of the Army. Troopships arrived periodically, loaded with hundreds of soldiers to reinforce the American units in the Philippines. But these ships had the more pressing priority of maintaining this trooplift, and were not available to detour to China to bring out the Marines. Admiral Hart and General MacArthur, from all accounts, had never been a smoothly coordinated team. Whether this circumstance had any effect on the decision that was made is not clear. MacArthur's cooperation may not have made much difference, in that the larger transports at his disposal were old and slow, as well as unarmed. Indeed, some were 535s, ex - American President Lines ships. The Army, however, at the time was chartering some fairly new and fast, albeit smaller, passenger ships under the Philippine flag; these included the *Don Esteban*, *Don Isidro*, *Legazpi*, and *Elcano*. These ships might have been ideal for the evacuation mission and could have left immediately for Shanghai. However, the Navy went ahead to acquire the ships it needed, largely on its own.

The Navy gunboats in the Yangtze River were out of the question as possible transports. The *Tutuila* was upriver at Chungking, the *Wake* was at Hankow, and the *Oahu* and *Luzon* were at Shanghai. In addition to being designated only for river service, these vessels were small. They would have enough trouble getting out of China on their own, and were in no position to evacuate any additional personnel.

Because of the number of Marines in Shanghai and the amount of equipment they would want to bring out, it was clear that more than one large ship would be needed. Two likely candidates were in the area. One was the *President Harrison* which had just arrived in Manila and had not even had time to discharge her cargo. The other was the *President Madison*, another 502 of the APL fleet, which had been in Manila a few days earlier and had gone on to Hong Kong to discharge her Shanghai passengers and cargo.

26

The last chance to evacuate safely the Marines from North China came and went with the venerable transport USS *Henderson*. (U.S. Naval Institute)

Sister ship to the *Harrison*, the *President Madison* shared in the evacuation of the 4th Marines from Shanghai. (American President Lines)

Captain Valdemar Nielsen of the *President Madison* was another long-time officer with the Dollar/APL fleet. (Valdemar Nielsen)

Commanding the Asiatic Fleet during a period of rapid disintegration was Admiral Thomas C. Hart. (U.S. Navy)

After the Marines had left Shanghai, RADM William A. Glassford departed with most of the remaining naval forces. (U.S. Navy)

All of the features in the design and history of the 502s now came into play in the Navy's decision to use the *President Harrison* and *President Madison*. The fact that they were built as transports, that they flew the Naval Reserve pennant, that their crews knew Shanghai intimately from many visits, that they belonged to a steamship company owned by the United States Government--all these factors made it clear that these were the ships to use.

Apparently no formal charter documents were drawn up in Manila; any such arrangements--if indeed they existed at all--were worked out among the Navy Department and Maritime Commission in Washington and the American President Lines in San Francisco. Admiral Hart's staff established procedures for radio communication with the two ships through the Cavite Naval Station, and issued the appropriate code books and instructions-- at least to the *Harrison*.

Although naval ships, primarily cruisers, were being used at this time to escort transports back and forth across the Pacific, none was made available for this operation, perhaps because the presence of a large surface warship in the East China Sea might be considered too provocative. Captain Pierson was told that four submarines would be available to escort the ships back to the Philippines, but that he could not count on direct contact with these vessels. The submarines assigned to the *Harrison* were the *Searaven* and *Seawolf*; those escorting the *Madison* were the *Perch* and *Permit*.

The *Harrison* left Manila on November 18th for Hong Kong where a hasty conversion job was to be carried out to prepare the ship for her new role as a troop ship. Since the ship would now be going to Shanghai after all, the passengers for that port were allowed to remain on board, rather than be disembarked at Hong Kong. With passengers aboard, the full crew of the ship remained on board.

In the meantime the *President Madison* was in Hong Kong where she had been discharging her Shanghai passengers and cargo. On her third day there the Captain was given a message through the APL office that he was to take the ship to Shanghai as quickly as possible to participate in the evacuation of 400 Marines.

Valdemar Nielsen, master of the *President Madison*, came from a maritime heritage as rich and colorful as that of Captain

Pierson of the *Harrison*. Born in 1899 in Denmark, he first went to sea in 1914 in Danish sailing vessels. During World War I he served in Norwegian, English, and Russian sailing ships. In 1921 he arrived in the United States in an American full-rigged ship, the *Arapahoe*, an ex-German ship seized by the U.S. Shipping Board. He obtained citizen's papers in 1923, and joined Dollar Line as a quartermaster in 1924, getting his initial mate's job later the same year. He had known Orel Pierson since 1924 when he had been a quartermaster in the *President Polk* when Pierson was third mate in that ship, and he had been aboard the *President Harrison* in 1926 when she hit Bonham Island. Nielsen's first command was the *President Van Buren* in 1932; he had been master of the *Madison* for more than a year at the start of the war.

Now, working with the disadvantage of getting all his information and instructions in roundabout fashion, Captain Nielsen quickly prepared for his new assignment. The APL port engineer in Hong Kong had been directed to acquire the materials for the conversion to a troop ship, largely lumber, and to load these materials onto the ship so that the work could be done in Shanghai. Arrangements were made with the Shanghai Engineering Company to accomplish this work in three days time upon the arrival of the *Madison*.

When the ship departed Hong Kong the captain was assured that additional lifejackets and rafts for the Marines would be brought up to Shanghai on the *Harrison*, several days behind the *Madison*, and that the American consul there would issue the necessary temporary certificate to permit the carrying of the extra passengers. At this point the mission had clearly become a military expedition, but it was still beset with the red tape of civilian passenger ship operation.

American President Lines even continued to promote the voyages. The Shanghai papers in their shipping news as late as the 27th carried APL sailing cards for the departure of the two ships. After that date the sailing cards carried no more listings for Shanghai departures, showing instead only Manila departures. However, at least two additional ships left after the papers ceased listing Shanghai departures, first a Dutch vessel and finally on December 3, 1941, the Chinese ship *Anhui*.

The *Harrison* arrived in Hong Kong on November 20th. In contrast to the *Madison* which still faced conversion work in

Shanghai, the *Harrison* had most of this work done during a three-day stay in the British crown colony. It consisted largely of the installation of wooden latrines in the after well deck, and the modification of the holds with bulkheads and piping. The conversion requirements included a toilet and shower for each 10 men, a separate galley and mess/recreation room for the troops, and space for the cots which were to be set up.

When the conversion work was nearly completed the *Harrison* left on the 23rd of November for Shanghai, three days away. On the passage north the officers on the ship, like their counterparts on the *Madison* well out ahead of them, took note of the heavy flow of Japanese troop ships and naval vessels moving south. It was an ominous sign that time was running out.

On November 26th, the *Harrison* steamed up the Yangtze, and riding the tide of the Whangpoo on up to Shanghai. She anchored below the city near the *Madison* which was busy with her conversion work after discharging cargo and passengers. After transferring the lifejackets, rafts, and other equipment to the *Madison*, the crew of the *Harrison* busied themselves in the same preparation activities, anticipating a quick turnaround and departure.

Elsewhere in the Far East, a significant departure was taking place on that day. Admiral Yamamoto's fleet was getting underway from Hitokappu Bay in the Kurile Islands. The Pearl Harbor attack force was on its way.

In Shanghai the Marines had made all their preparations and were ready to go. Aware that they had served in what was considered one of the very best duty stations in the Marine Corps, the officers and men of the 4th Regiment knew that it was now time to say goodbye to the good life of garrison duty in this most cosmopolitan city in the world. The people of the large business community of Shanghai, also realizing that the Marines had to leave, wondered fearfully about the future. For the last two years large numbers of dependents of Europeans and Americans working in Shanghai had been brought out to the relative safety of the Philippines, Australia and the States. Indeed, the American President Lines had benefitted from this exodus.

In the International Settlement the United States Marines had become as much of an institution as was the extraterritoriality they defended. The Marines has originally come to China to protect American lives and property during the Boxer Insurrection of 1898. Through the years they had continued to carry out that responsibility by means of a small but influential presence in critical places and times, such as aboard American freight and passenger vessels on the Yangtze where they deterred the bandits and pirates who preyed on such commerce. But they had done more than just police the countryside; when European nations were ready to carve up the country into foreign enclaves, the presence of U.S. Marines had been a stabilizing factor, an extension of the American open-door policy of helping to develop China without acquiring and operating any of the foreign concessions extracted by other nations.

These Marines had first come to the International Settlement in 1927 on Navy transports, the old Hog Islander *Chaumont* and the *Henderson*, along with the *President Grant*, a 535 of the Dollar-controlled American Mail Line. For the most part, they had enjoyed the high life of Shanghai where garrison duty had such benefits as servants even for enlisted men, liberty which began at noon, good cheap whiskey, and many other sophisticated pleasures to be tasted. The purchasing power of their slim pay was enhanced by the judicious use of money changers who bid monthly on the conversion rate of the American payroll into Chinese dollars. But in 1932 the Marines had been called out into sandbagged positions on the streets to protect the International Settlement from hostilities between Japanese and Chinese forces which had broken out across Soochow Creek. In 1937, when Japan occupied China following the Marco Polo Bridge Incident, the Marines again took up defensive positions during attacks on Shanghai. Throughout the difficult four years of the Japanese occupation a *modus vivendi* had developed; the Marines hung on tenaciously to their role as a buffer between aggressive Japanese aspirations and Shanghai's determination to survive as the unique city it was.

Following the outbreak of the war in Europe in 1939 a chain of circumstances eliminated other foreign troops from any role as co-protectors of the Settlement. Eventually the Marines provided the only military force to counter Japanese territorial aspirations toward the city. Because of Italy's role in the Rome-Berlin-Tokyo axis, troops of that country were of no value to Anglo-American commercial interests in Shanghai. The French garrison in the city had been neutralized on orders from the Vichy government after the fall of France in 1940. Although their naval vessels were still in evidence, British ground forces had been withdrawn shortly thereafter in order to assist in the defense of Singapore. Thus, U.S. Marines were the only defenders of the fragile status quo in Shanghai in late 1941.

The nostalgia and sentimentality of the city's feelings toward the Marines were to be expressed in a number of ways during the several days while the *Madison* and *Harrison* were in port. In the best tradition of Shanghai, the departure of the Marines called for a party. The British novelist J. G. Ballard, who grew up in the city, writing later in *Empire of the Sun* referred to "the 50-year-long party that had been Shanghai." Now, on the evening of November 26, 1941, the city gave one of its last such affairs to bid farewell to the Marines, a party hosted by and at the American Club.

Prominent guests included Rear Admiral William A. Glassford, head of Navy forces in Shanghai, Colonel Samuel L. Howard, Commanding Officer of the 4th Marine Regiment, and Captain Valdemar Nielsen of the *Madison*. Because the *Harrison* had arrived earlier that day and he had been on the bridge of that ship for many hours, Captain Orel Pierson did not attend.

Only a few junior officers and some enlisted men were in uniform. Otherwise the event was undistinguishable from other civilian social affairs, with drinks, a buffet, and dancing. The mood was merry, but not boisterous. In later years Captain Nielsen recalled the evening clearly, especially his meeting with the military leaders.

> *During my conversation with the Admiral he asked me when my ship would finish discharging her cargo. I informed him that we had finished some time earlier, and now we were waiting to complete the Marine accommodations; otherwise we were ready to sail.*
>
> *I thought the Admiral was going to blow his top. "I have been misinformed," he said. Then he hollered, "Sam, come over here." When the Colonel appeared the Admiral said, "Captain Nielsen has just informed me his ship is ready to embark. Are you ready?"*
>
> *The Colonel replied, "Accommodations on the ship are not quite complete," to which the Admiral said, "The*

*Marines are very handy men; they can complete the
unfinished work on the way. Forget about the parade.
I suggest you commence embarkation at 0800 tomor-
row, and we will set a sailing time on the afternoon
high water tide. I can see the handwriting on the
wall. It is later than we think."*

*The Colonel hesitated, and then replied, "Yes, sir.
Can do. Will do."*

Perhaps Colonel Howard had hesitated because he had
promised his men they would march out of Shanghai in style--
in a parade. In any case, after the Admiral had expressed his
intentions, many of the officers left the party and went back to
their preparations.

With the end of the social interlude it was time for each of
the three commanders to return to the job of preparing his
command for the busy hours ahead: Nielsen to his venerable
502, Glassford to his splinter fleet of gunboats, and Howard to
his impatient troops. For the Marines it was time to put away
the dress uniforms and mufti of life in the International Settlement, and to take up instead field uniforms and packs. Running
through the minds of some must have been the words of a
popular song from a 1937 movie which romanticized the adven-
turous life of the Marines: "It may be Shanghai, farewell and
goodbye." However, the final line, "We're shovin' right off for
home again," was not an accurate description of the impending
departure of these Marines.

November 27th dawned bleak and rainy in Shanghai. It was
the American Thanksgiving Day. In a sense, the Marines had
much for which to be thankful; they were pulling out of a
dangerous situation. But it was to be the last such occasion for
several years on which they would have much reason to be
thankful for what life had brought to them.

The rain solved Colonel Howard's problem concerning the
parade. It would now be impractical to march the men through
the city to the landing with full equipment. So the men of the
2nd Battalion and half of the Regimental Headquarters and
Service Company, under the command of Lieutenant Colonel
Donald Curtis, were transported to the docks in a very un-
Marine-like fashion: in a fleet of sleek double-decker buses. The
Japanese troops offered no resistance. At the landing on the

The 4th Marines marched through the business of district of Shanghai on their final day in China. (Carla Allan)

Colonel Samuel L. Howard led the 4th Marines onto the Shanghai Bund for their sentimental journey out of China. (Carla Allan)

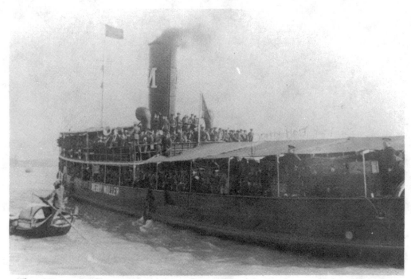

The *Merry Moller* was used to ferry the 4th Marines to the *President Harrison* waiting downriver. (Carla Allan)

Leaving the *Harrison* at Olongapo, the 4th Marines were soon to be engaged heavily in combat. (Louis Duncan)

Bund, correspondents and photographers had assembled in spite of the rain to record the event. In a brief ceremony local officials thanked Colonel Curtis and proclaimed Chinese-American friendship; the poncho-clad Marines then filed aboard the *Merry Moller* and other tenders to be ferried out to the *Madison*, a mile downstream. In the absence of their own band which was in the second detachment leaving the next day, the Marines were treated to the music of a band from a Chinese orphanage. When the strains of Auld Lang Syne wafted across the murky waters of the Whangpoo, tears were shed profusely by the Chinese and Russian cabaret girls who had come down to the customs jetty for the farewell. Even among the men it was a misty-eyed experience. Thus, the Thanksgiving Day embarkation, although not as dramatic as the one to come on the following day, was a memorable and successful withdrawal from Shanghai for half the regiment.

At about 1600 hours that afternoon, with troops and some outbound civilian passengers embarked, the *Madison* got underway for the naval station at Olongapo, Philippine Islands, and for Manila beyond. Even though the accommodations were primitive and incomplete, the passage would prove to be quiet and uneventful, requiring no special military preparedness on board. The only real surprise occurred when, unknowingly, the ship arrived at her rendezvous point, The Saddles, the offshore islands marking the southern approaches to the Yangtze, before her submarine escort was on station. In a curious commentary on Japanese-American relations at this critical time, the Japanese Navy provided an escort of four destroyers which fell in astern of the *Madison* for the first part of the voyage, in lieu of the submarines.

That same day, November 27th, the Navy Department sent a warning to fleet commanders in the Pacific, saying in part, "This dispatch is to be considered a war warning... An aggressive move by Japan is expected within the next few days." This message went on to say that the hostile move would probably be an amphibious operation against either the Philippines or Malaya, or possibly Borneo. Admiral Hart saw the message in Manila where he discussed it with the ever-optimistic General MacArthur, but it is not clear if Admiral Glassford saw it in Shanghai. Whether he did or not was largely moot, inasmuch as he planned to withdraw his tiny fleet as soon as the *Harrison* left the following day.

Perhaps Admiral Glassford did see the war alert, because at about 1000 on the 27th--even as the *Madison* was still loading--he ordered Colonel Howard to step up the loading of the remaining supplies and equipment to be transported on the *Harrison*. Throughout the rest of the day these supplies were trucked to the docks for lightering out to the ship. Loading priorities as worked out by regimental quartermaster Major Reginald H. Ridgely Jr., were, in descending order: ammunition, field equipment, medical supplies, rations, motor transport, clothing, miscellaneous, and household effects.

The imminent departure of the last American troops from Shanghai now triggered a wave of harrassment on the part of Japanese troops in the city. Why the Japanese at this late date would want to impede the withdrawal of their strongest adversary is not clear, unless they wanted an opportunity to capture remaining American Marines within a few hours after the start of the war.

American intelligence had indicated for months that the Japanese Army was anxious to take over the International Settlement, even by force if necessary. Reportedly, however, the Japanese Navy view prevailed instead; that service wanted to manufacture an "incident"--a favorite ploy of the Japanese in overrunning China--to justify action against the Americans. By their level-headed and professional behavior the Marines had judiciously avoided being drawn into such an incident.

Now, as the Japanese instituted a number of delaying actions, the Marines reacted as indulgently yet resourcefully as they could. Colonel Howard, later in a post-war report, described the situation.

> *All supplies had to pass through the Japanese Sector on the way to the Customs dock. About 3:00 p.m., November 27, they closed the Garden Bridge over Soochow Creek to traffic and our trucks were delayed nearly an hour before contact could be made with the Japanese Admiral to get this bridge reopened to traffic. Customs officials ostensibly at the instigation of the Japanese were insistent that our supplies pass through the Custom House, but we ignored such orders and loaded them on lighters. The Japanese instigated three*

34

strikes during the night by the laborers loading the lighters.

When daylight came to Shanghai on the 28th most of the equipment and gear of the Marines had been stowed in the holds of the *Harrison,* in spite of the work stoppages during the night. Now the troops could be embarked directly from the Bund in the International Settlement, rather than having to cross into Japanese-controlled territory below Soochow Creek where the supplies had been loaded. Rain no longer fell, but it was a gloomy, overcast day.

Colonel Howard could now make good on his promise of a parade. At 0900 the 1st Battalion and the other half of the Headquarters and Service Company fell in at the staging area near their barracks on Ferry Road, and began the three-mile trek through the city to the Bund. Leading the march along with his staff was Colonel Howard, the erect, graying 50-year-old commanding officer. He was followed by the regimental band, playing such marches as "The Stars and Stripes Forever." Lining the route along Nanking and Bubbling Well Roads and the streets of the shopping districts were tens of thousands of people waving American and Chinese flags. Soon the sun came out, brightening the day.

Accounts differ as to the mood of the crowds. Marine histories speak of "cheering people," but the Associated Press account in the *New York Times* said, "There were few smiles and no cheers." Perhaps both perceptions were accurate in their own way. One observer, a young Dutch woman, noted later that the mood varied considerably from place to place, depending on the ethnicity of the people at a given point and their degree of involvement with the Marines. As one of those deeply involved, she remembers that "Outwardly we cheered, smiled, and waved, but inside we knew we'd never see them again. And we didn't..."

As the troops passed, the crowd filled the street behind the Marines, surging on with them toward the river. Near the racetrack a dixieland band fell in at the end of the column. The response of the people of Shanghai was a remarkable display of affection for the Leathernecks.

Possibly no other withdrawal of a modern military force, particularly an occupation force, has ever been carried out so dramatically and with such intense public response. Arrivals of military forces have been accompanied by parades and enthusiastic mass welcomes, as in Paris upon the arrival of the AEF in 1917 or the liberating American troops in World War II. But this kind of emotional withdrawal, in the face of certain captivity as an alternative, simply does not occur elsewhere in modern military history.

At the landing on the Bund a large official delegation gathered to bid farewell to the unit, including members of the Municipal Council, foreign consuls and diplomatic representatives, the commanding officers of all military units, including even the Japanese, and the heads of many civic organizations.

According to Marines who were there, media coverage of the event was extensive, with dozens of newspaper and magazine correspondents, photographers, and newsreel cameramen present. However, while the story of the Shanghai evacuation was reported by the wire services, photographic evidence of the remarkable event seems to be rather scarce today.

After the parade, the speeches were an anti-climax. Following several hours of shuttling back and forth between the dock and the ship, the tenders succeeded in loading the last of the troops. At 1400 hours the *President Harrison* weighed anchor and started down the Whangpoo which was lined with flag-waving people. At Woosung she reached the main channel of the Yangtze and headed for the open sea. An era had come to an end for the Marine Corps, and the party was over for Shanghai.

While the *Harrison* had been getting underway, the American gunboat *Wake* arrived in Shanghai from her station at Hankow, up the Yangtze. This vessel, considered too small and frail to make the passage to the Philippines, was to be stripped of both personnel and equipment during the balance of the day so she could be left in Shanghai after the departure of the other gunboats, there to serve as a communications center for remaining American interests through a skeleton crew including local Naval Reservists. Within 10 days these men would become the first American prisoners of war of World War II.

That night, shortly after midnight, the rest of the American naval forces in Shanghai pulled out. The gunboats *Oahu* and *Luzon*, with Admiral Glassford embarked in the latter vessel departed Shanghai for the perilous passage to Manila. The fourth gunboat, the *Tutuila*, was so far upriver at Chungking that it was considered impossible to bring her down the Yangtze and out in time, so she was turned over to the Chinese Nationalist government and her crew repatriated by air. The fifth gunboat in China, the *Mindanao*, was at Hong Kong; she waited cautiously before starting for Manila, primarily to see how the *Oahu* and *Luzon* were faring.

The remarkable story of the gunboat evacuation is told in Captain W. G. Winslow's book, *The Fleet the Gods Forgot, The United States Asiatic Fleet in World War II.* For Admiral Glassford, who hauled down his flag and formally dissolved the Yangtze River Patrol upon arrival in Manila, the difficult voyage compounded by a late-season typhoon was the first of a number of retreats he would make to the south as the Asiatic Fleet began to recede as a fighting force. It must have been a difficult moment for the 55-year-old admiral who had once won the Distinguished Service Medal for keeping afloat the destroyer he commanded after it had been rammed by the *Aquitania* during World War I.

But aboard the *President Harrison* morale was high; the longtime civilian liner, although she still had some passengers on board, was at last a military transport, enjoying a heady moment of glory as an heroic ship of the Asiatic Fleet, by function if not by formal credentials. Unbeknownst to those on board, she had now acquired the submarine escort, all four of the boats including the two the *Madison* was supposed to have had. Unlike her sister ship which made the passage with no special precautions, the *Harrison* took on the look and feel of a fighting ship. The Marines lashed .50 caliber machine-guns to the rails topside, and blackout procedures were enforced.

The passage to the Philippines was, nevertheless, a safe one. Although Japanese ships and aircraft monitored the progress of the *Harrison*, she was allowed to proceed without harrassment. It was not a comfortable trip for the Marines, however, because there were not enough bunks to go around; some men slept on deck in sleeping bags. Midway across, the four submarines surfaced and showed their American flags before departing, providing both reassurance and a thrill for the crew, the troops, and the few passengers on the ship. After a three-and-a-half day trip, during which the Marines shifted into summer uniforms, the *Harrison* arrived at Subic Bay.

The *Madison* had already disembarked her troops at the naval station at Olongapo, and gone on to Manila. Now on December 1st the Marines from the *Harrison* were lightered ashore onto American-controlled territory. Quickly, they began to organize themselves into a different kind of fighting unit, one that Admiral Hart would later describe as "the strongest infantry regiment in the Philippines." Strength notwithstanding, the entire unit was soon to be captured on Bataan and Corregidor.

At this point several uncoordinated and indecisive actions on the part of Hart's staff took place, actions that may well have been responsible for the ultimate capture of the *Harrison* on the next leg of her odyssey. Although Hart's post-war narrative reported that the "weapons, munitions, field equipment, and all supplies" of the 4th Marines were unloaded at Olongapo, Marine accounts say that "only a few supplies were unloaded at the naval station." The latter version cites two reasons why Hart made this decision: the need to get the ship down the coast and through the Corregidor minefield in daylight hours, and the desirability of landing only their field equipment so that the troops could get into the field as soon as possible and begin conditioning themselves for combat.

Although confirmation of these reports is difficult to obtain, it appears that the *Harrison* went on to Manila, arriving on December 2nd, where the heavy equipment was unloaded to be trucked back to Olongapo. This movement was particularly ironic because within a few days the 1st Battalion was brought back down the coast by tug, lighter, and truck to Mariveles at the head of the Bataan Peninsula, opposite Corregidor. The trip to Manila was also costly in time, because had the *Harrison* been turned around and sent north from Olongapo on the 1st of December she might have had time enough to reach North China; instead, she was not ready to leave Manila until the 4th, and she had a longer trip by half a day when leaving from the latter point.

This speculation is best understood in the context of what took place in Manila during the first four days of December. Both the *Madison* and *Harrison* were in port, back from their trooplift missions. Using this opportunity to discharge fully and to rearrange their cargoes, both ships were getting organized to resume the next leg of their interrupted voyages. Inasmuch as the *Madison* had more Singapore cargo than did the *Harrison*, she was released from Navy service and allowed to continue her voyage to that port and then back to the States. The *Harrison* after discharging and/or transferring all her passengers and cargo, was detained for the time being.

The return of the *Madison* to the United States became in its own right an incredible, albeit unheralded voyage, as remarkable as that of any ship during the frantic early days of the war. En route to Singapore, she stopped off on December 7th at Balikpapan in Borneo for fuel. There she picked up a number of Dutch women and children whom she took to Sourabaya in Sumatra. There, other refugees including American women and children were picked up, along with strategic cargo. Because of war conditions, the ship avoided Singapore; she worked her way out of Asian waters, across the Indian Ocean, and around the Cape of Good Hope. Finally, seven months and four days after leaving San Francisco and after sailing 47,340 miles, the *President Madison* arrived in New York--much to the surprise of American President Lines officials who had long since given her up for dead. This unusual voyage was described in an article in the *Saturday Evening Post* in July 1942. It was written by J. B. Magruder, a merchant marine deck cadet who was repatriated at Bombay. Other passengers boarding at this port included the crew of the Navy gunboat *Tutuila* who had been airlifted to India from China.

According to Captain Nielsen, Tokyo Rose had at various times reported the ship captured off Shanghai, torpedoed in the South China Sea, and torpedoed in the Bay of Bengal. Nielsen blamed "stupid" Navy operation orders for several close calls, saying "If I had not disobeyed those orders Tokyo Rose reports would have been correct."

After this longest and last of all round-the-world voyages of the American President Lines, the *President Madison* was requisitioned for Navy service as the transport *Kenmore*, first designated AK 221 and then AP 62. After a career of about 21 months in that role, she was converted to a hospital ship, becoming the USS *Refuge*. She carried that status until the end of the war when she would again cross paths with the survivors of the *Harrison*.

Back in Manila, the remaining few days of the career of the *President Harrison* as an American ship were in the hands of the staff of Commander, Asiatic Fleet. Admiral Hart's planners were now hurriedly organizing another rescue mission--this time to bring out the embassy guards from North China. In his strangely terse "narrative," Hart later offered only a two-sentence comment about that effort: "One of the President Line ships was turned around as quickly as possible and sailed for Chinwangtao. She never arrived there."

Chapter 4

The Expedition That Failed

"The United States Asiatic Fleet seldom tasted victory. It drank the cup of defeat to the bitter dregs." So wrote Samuel E. Morison in his monumental series, *History of U.S. Naval Operations in World War II*.

Although the war had not yet begun, Admiral Hart for the moment had achieved a rare victory for the Asiatic Fleet in rescuing the 4th Marines from China. However, the task of bringing out the more than 200 Marines in North China had not been concurrently addressed; it still lay ahead.

Most of the records of the Asiatic Fleet were later lost when it ceased to exist upon the Navy's abandonment of the Philippines early in 1942. Accordingly, it is impossible to learn much at this late date about how Admiral Hart's staff made the decision to send the *President Harrison* to Chinwangtao, and why that decision was made after the return of the ship from Shanghai.

Inasmuch as the authorization to evacuate all personnel from China came on November 10th, and the *Harrison* did not return to Manila until December 4th, one can obviously conclude that there were three weeks available to look for another ship while the two 502s were making the Shanghai trip. About November 18th a Shanghai newspaper reported, "Although the exact date of the departure of the Marines is still a closely-guarded secret the *China Press* learned from authoritative sources that the first batch will leave here on Tuesday next, while those stationed in Peiping and Tientsin will be carried direct to Manila from Chinwangtao on an American President Lines vessel, now used as an Army transport. The vessel, it was learned, will not call at Shanghai."

This report bears examination. The first part of this speculation turned out to be quite accurate, although it was not Tuesday next but Thursday next when the first contingent of Marines actually departed Shanghai. Perhaps the second part of the report was also based on good information; in that case, another ship had apparently been lined up at that time. If it were indeed an APL ship being used as an Army transport, the possibilities would be reduced to only a few ships.

One could have been the army transport *Willard Holbrook,* the former *President Taft* which had been the previous command of Captain Pierson of the *Harrison.* She had been running between the West Coast and Manila in the trooplift, but had probably left Manila on her way back to the States before the evacuation authorization came on November 10th, inasmuch as she was known to have departed Honolulu, westbound, on November 30th. So it seems unlikely that she would have been available for use in mid-November in Manila.

The *President Taylor* had also been in Manila early in November, but had probably left before the 10th. Also, she had no ties to the Army at that time.

Another possibility might have been the *President Grant* which arrived in Manila just before the war broke out. Although the *Grant* was later to be allocated to the Army as a troop ship by the War Shipping Administration, she apparently was not recognized as an Army vessel in 1941. She would not have been available in Manila until early in December. The *President Coolidge* had apparently also been in Manila in November, but she, too, had no identity as an Army vessel at that time, although maritime sources earlier in 1941 had reported her acquisition by the Army Transport Service, a report that was quickly denied by APL.

A final possibility was the *President Pierce*, a 535 formerly used by APL in trans-Pacific service, which had become the USAT *Hugh L. Scott* in 1941, later to be turned over to the Navy in 1942. She had been in Manila during the latter part of November, and was about a third of the way across the Pacific, homeward bound in the company of the *President Coolidge* and the cruiser *Louisville* at the time of Pearl Harbor. The *Scott* seems to be the ship that comes closest to the definition in the *China Press* and the one whose presence in Manila in mid to late November made her a likely candidate for selection. But, as noted earlier, the Army was apparently not willing to give up a troop ship to the Navy for the Chinwangtao venture.

Three critical weeks had passed. If, indeed, there had been any joint Army-Navy effort to free up a transport, there was no evidence of any outcome; no ship had been produced. It is curious that the headquarters of the Asiatic Fleet had worried about the continued presence of the Marine troops in China for more than a year, and yet had given little thought to how these men would be evacuated when final approval to do so came from Washington. During 1940 the Navy itself had acquired a dozen transports, and almost twice that many in 1941. In addition, six old "four-piper" destroyers had been converted to APDs or fast transports, each capable of sealifting one third of a Marine battalion at 25 knots. Thus, 33 transports were in Navy service at the start of the war--twice as many as in Army service-- and yet the Navy seemingly had nothing available in the Far East to move Marines in late 1941.

One is tempted to ask, where were the Navy's transports and what were they doing? Twenty-five were operating out of the East Coast of the United States, and eight were in the Pacific, only three of which were west of Pearl Harbor: the *Chaumont* and *Republic* trying to reach Manila, and the *Burrows* serving Johnston, Midway, and Wake Islands. The Army, too, had only a few regular troop ships in the Southwest Pacific. Clearly, the largest transport fleet in the Far East was that of the American President Lines.

Finally the Navy was forced to act. By this time only the *Harrison* remained as a possible candidate for the mission since the *Madison* had been allowed to leave for Southeast Asia.

Captain Pierson recalled many years later how he received his orders to go to Chinwangtao:

> *On the night before leaving Manila a ranking naval officer on Admiral Hart's staff while sitting in my cabin--and for my ears only--said to me, "We want you to do this task for us. We think you can pull it off, and are the only one available. We would like to get our men out. We know that all hell is going to break out soon in these waters; we just don't know where or when."*

This officer had come on board to deliver personally the code books the ship would need to stay in radio contact with the Cavite Naval Station. No written orders were delivered to the ship--only the oral instructions, "Proceed to Chinwangtao and bring out the Marines." The transaction was between Captain

Pierson as a Naval Reserve officer and the Navy; the American President Lines apparently did not enter into the agreement. It seems clear that Captain Pierson had the option of refusing to make the trip, but chose to go.

No arrangements were made for any escort vessels. Why the Navy did not furnish the same type of submarine escort that had been provided on the Shanghai evacuation was not clear. There were 29 submarines in the Philippines at the time, only three of which were out of service; thus, it was not a question of the unavailability of vessels. It is possible--and not difficult--to conclude that Admiral Hart was writing off the entire expedition as hopeless. The only resource provided to the ship in case of a crisis was through the fatuous advice from the Navy, "Try to make Vladivostock."

There was little time for additional preparations. The troop facilities from the Shanghai trip were still in place, so no special work was needed to accommodate the Marines. All passengers and cargo were put ashore. However, the dozens of steward's department crewmembers who were not needed now to handle the self-contained Marines were inexplicably all left aboard. Clara Main, the stewardess, was offered the opportunity to get off the ship, but she elected to stay. Thus, the ship still functioned as a full-service passenger liner as she prepared to sail north on the eve of war into the waters of the East China and Yellow Seas, long controlled by the Japanese.

As a gesture of its responsibility as a steamship company toward those travelling on its vessels, American President Lines sent aboard a passenger agent who had been recalled from leave in the States and had just arrived in Manila. E. S. Wise had been the APL passenger agent in Shanghai at the time that office was closed during the summer of 1941. While on leave he had been ordered back to the Far East to, by his recollection, reopen the Shanghai office, or, more likely, according to company histories, to serve as passenger agent in Manila. In any case, upon his arrival in Manila on the *President Grant*, Wise was instructed to take a small suitcase and go aboard the *Harrison* for a trip of a "few days" to assist in the transporting of the Marines.

The departure of the *Harrison* was set for the morning of Thursday, December 4, 1941, Manila time. Although it was supposed to be a secret, the sailing, as well as its destination, was a matter of common knowledge in the bars of the city the previous evening. The Japanese, too, knew of the mission, according to what Captain Pierson later learned from his captors.

Chinwangtao was about 1,700 miles away, almost a five day trip for a 502. Captain Pierson had every reason to be apprehensive; in spite of his many years visiting the major ports of the Far East he had never been to Chinwangtao. On this trip he was destined once again not to reach that port.

Chinwangtao, like Shanghai, was one of the "treaty ports" of China, but it was much less known than its flamboyant counterpart to the south. Developed by the British under a turn-of-the-century concession, it was largely a coal port. Its primary advantage over the other ports on the Gulf of Bohai was its relatively deep ice-free water, making it a year-round port for larger vessels with passengers and cargo for Tientsin, 140 miles southwest along the coast, and Peking, 175 miles inland to the west. It was the most northerly of China's major ports; from the U.S. Marine Corps facility there the Great Wall of China could be seen.

The Marines had come to North China in 1898, even before the Boxer Insurrection. While the American Army had done the bulk of the garrison duty there prior to 1938, three Marine detachments remained in 1941: the embassy guards in Peking, the legation guards in Tientsin, and a small unit at Camp Holcomb at Chinwangtao which was responsible for loading and unloading supplies for the larger units. In overall command of all North China Marines was Colonel William W. Ashurst, in Peking where 141 men were stationed; the Tientsin detachment of 49 men was commanded by Major Luther A. Brown; and the Camp Holcomb group of 14 men was headed by Second Lieutenant Richard M. Huizenga.

Aware that they would soon be pulling out, the North China Marines were busy shipping their gear to Camp Holcomb in anticipation of the arrival of the *President Harrison* on December 10th or 11th. For them, as with their buddies in Shanghai, the good life was ending.

In early December each man shipped his personal gear to Chinwangtao except for his rifle and 60 rounds of ammunition or his .45 caliber pistol and 21 rounds. On December 4th Admiral Hart radioed, "Destroy all codes, confidential and secret material except DITOF [a confidential radio code]. Report destruction immediately. When ordered, report destruction of DITOF by single word 'Jabberwocky' in clear." Captain John A. White, the executive officer at Tientsin, personally supervised the burning of the aluminum cylinder codes.

The personal property of the Marines moved by train from Peking and Tientsin to the railroad siding at Camp Holcomb for ultimate shipment on the *President Harrison*. Amid the personal belongings of 200 Marines, several boxes were also sent to Chinwangtao for the *Harrison*. These boxes were reportedly of incredible importance in that they contained the bones of Peking Man.

Peking Man, originally designated as *Sinanthropus Pekenensis*, was an important anthropological find made in 1927 at Chou-k'ou-tien cave near Peking. A small number of bones of this primitive man dating from the middle Pleistocene era had been assembled at the Peking Union Medical College, an institution sponsored by the Rockefeller Foundation. With the threat of large-scale war, Chinese officials had decided to send the bones out of the country for safe keeping. Two packing boxes were filled by Claire Taschdjian, assistant to the researcher in charge of the project. One contained the bones of Peking Man; the other held bones from a later period from the same general excavation area.

The medical school staff, knowing of the impending departure of the Marines, sent the two boxes to Colonel Ashurst at Marine headquarters in Peking. Ashurst recalled later:

> *During November 1941 several boxes were accepted by me from officials of the Peking Union Medical College for shipment to the United States. These boxes were shipped together with other property belonging to the Marine Detachment, Peking, China, via rail to Chinwangtao, China, in late November or early December in freight cars guarded by U.S. Marine Corps personnel. These materials remained in the cars at Chinwangtao awaiting shipment in the U.S.S. [sic] President Harrison to Manila, Philippines, and were so located when the war started on December 8, 1941.*

According to some accounts, before the collection left Peking, Colonel Ashurst had ordered it transferred from the wooden crates to regulation Marine footlockers, and consigned them to the care of Lieutenant (junior grade) William T. Foley, the unit's medical officer who was due to return to the United States as soon as he reached the Philippines. He, in turn, would deliver the famous fossils to the American Museum of Natural History in New York City. Other accounts speak of pine, or redwood, boxes on which Colonel Ashurst had his name stenciled.

Apparently, several footlockers with Dr. Foley's name on them and at least one with Colonel Ashurst's name on it did arrive at Camp Holcomb in Chinwangtao, but accounts of this shipment do not make clear which of these footlockers was supposed to contain the bones. As will be evident in a later chapter of this book, the fact that no person could ever swear to having seen the bones put into a footlocker or box with either Dr. Foley's or Colonel Ashurst's name on it meant that all the later speculation about the disposition of the footlockers or boxes, no matter how well reasoned, was of questionable value. Thus, the mystery of Peking Man began even before his bones disappeared. In any case, the fate of about 200 men and possibly that of a great scientific treasure, awaited the arrival of the *President Harrison* in Chinwangtao.

On Sunday night, December 7th, some of the Marine officers at Tientsin were entertained at a festive farewell party hosted by the White Russian colony in that city. Grateful that another peaceful Sunday had passed--since a common feeling in the Far East was that any Japanese attack would occur on a Sunday morning to take advantage of a collective hangover for American forces--and grateful that they would soon be leaving for a safer area, the Marines partied late into the night. Dr. Foley arrived by rickshaw at his quarters at 4 a.m. as the clear, cold air dipped to 40 degrees below zero. He was to be awakened much earlier than he had planned, with the realization that, after a peaceful Sunday in the Far East, the Japanese could still start a war on a Sunday by going east of the International Date Line to do it.

Eight hundred miles to the south, the *President Harrison* spent December 7th steaming up the East China Sea. The numerous day workers in the crew, particularly in the large steward's department, were enjoying their day off. The passage from the Philippines had been relatively quiet. During the first 24 hours, while still in the South China Sea, the ship had unknowingly passed Admiral Glassford's two gunboats, the *Oahu* and the *Luzon*, making for Manila at the end of their stormy passage from Shanghai. Farther along, the watch officers on the bridge of the *Harrison*--First Mate Jon Thuesen, Second Mate Matthew Sullivan, and Third Mate Sydney Olsen--took note of the heavy volume of Japanese shipping moving to the south.

On the evening of December 7th, the *Harrison* experienced her first encounter with a Japanese vessel. As Captain Pierson remembered the incident,

> *Just after dark we were approached by some sort of a craft which flashed "stop." We stopped but, as this craft did not come alongside and we were an American ship proceeding upon a peaceful mission, I decided to ignore him entirely and proceed upon our way. As we were faster than this craft we soon outdistanced him.*
>
> *Long afterwards while in a camp in Japan I learned that this was a small Japanese naval craft which had stopped the SS **Elsie Moeller** just before dark, and then seeing us coming up on the horizon had left the **Elsie** and proceeded in our direction. The captain of the **Elsie** had left Chinwangtao with a load of coal for Shanghai, but had been ordered to make all haste for Singapore instead. He had been told that we were bound [for Chinwangtao] and that no doubt he would meet up with us somewhere along the way. Being a China coast skipper and knowing our ships, he recognized us.*

Passenger agent Wise recalled seeing two vessels approach the ship during this particular evening, and that they directed their searchlights on the *Harrison*. The incident proved to be relatively inconsequential, but it did provide the Japanese with a reliable position, course, and speed for the ship.

One of the radio operators, Roy Madden, in later years told a bizarre story about the *Harrison* receiving a message late on the night of the 7th from a White Russian radio station indicating that the ship would be captured. Madden claimed that the *Harrison* then sent a message to "KRS" announcing the start of the war, 24 hours before Pearl Harbor, but that message was disregarded. No confirmation for this weird and inconsistent story can be found.

The new day of Monday, December 8th, began quietly along the China coast. The trackline projected for the *Harrison* that day called for her to round The Saddles, the cluster of offshore islands that mark the easternmost extension of China into the East China Sea, and to make for Shantung Peninsula as the next landfall on the mainland. Although the first part of the night had passed uneventfully, the watch on the bridge had been particularly alert to the navigational hazards represented by a large number of rocky islands inshore to the west, including Bonham Island where the *Harrison* had grounded in 1926. Ironically, these islands at the turn of the century had been favored by a number of prominent Americans, including the influential Admiral Mahan, as the site of a China coast naval base, but the idea for the base was abandoned with the adoption of the "Open Door" policy by the United States.

Now, for Third Mate Olsen on the 8-12 watch, Second Mate Sullivan on the 12-4, and First Mate Thuesen on the 4-8, accurate piloting was required, using the few but important lighthouses along this coast. Traffic was also a problem at this critical turning point on the coast, particularly junks with dim oil-burning lights or no lights at all. Like other merchant ships of that era, the *Harrison* had no radar.

At about 0230 on the 8th of December the ship passed the lighthouse on North Saddle Island to port, and set a course of 328° for Shaweishan Island Light, about 40 miles across the mouth of the Yangtze. A moon, only a few days past full, lingered in the western sky.

Five time zones to the east and a day earlier on the calendar, Japanese carrier aircraft were now within sight of Oahu. Within a few minutes the infamous attack on Pearl Harbor would begin, sending events reeling at an out-of-control pace for American forces in the Pacific, and for the *President Harrison* in particular.

At 0258, China coast time, the message was sent out from Pearl Harbor: "Air raid, Pearl Harbor. This is no drill." In Manila Admiral Hart was awakened at 0300 by an aide, Marine Lieutenant Colonel William T. Clement. Hart quickly sent a terse message to units of his Asiatic Fleet: "Japan started hostilities. Govern yourselves accordingly."

At about three thirty, the *Harrison*'s midwatch radio officer,

Jasper Treadway, heard a plain language broadcast with news of the Pearl Harbor attack, and awoke the captain. This message may have come from the Navy radio station at Cavite; while the Navy would normally use code in messages to its ships, there was no need for secrecy on this information since the Japanese knew only too well what had happened.

Now came the moment of truth, the time for Captain Pierson to make an important decision affecting the ship and her crew. It certainly made no sense to make further efforts to reach Chinwangtao; all of coastal China was in Japanese hands. The Navy's suggested port of refuge, Vladivostock in Russia, was equally unthinkable; while it was perhaps a half-day closer than Manila, reaching it would entail going through the Korea Straits, close to the Japanese home islands. Returning to the south might buy a little time, but with the major thrust of Japan's aggression expected to be in that direction, it seemed certain that those waters would be full of Japanese ships. The only possible escape route at the moment lay to the southeast, through the passages between the scattered islands of the Ryukyus chain, north of Okinawa. While these islands were Japanese, they were not heavily fortified, and it might be possible to slip through them to reach the open ocean beyond.

As long as escape was still a possibility, that alternative seemed to represent the only choice. With three and a half hours of darkness remaining, Captain Pierson ordered a course to the southeast, hoping that he could get far enough offshore to escape detection, but aware that it would take more than a day of steaming to reach the island chain. He was also aware that, thanks to a parsimonious APL port engineer in Manila, he had only enough fuel for about eight days of steaming and that Hawaii was 11 days away; even Midway Island was nine days away.

At daybreak the ship was still fleeing toward the southeast. Ed Wise, the passenger agent, awoke to find sunlight steaming through the porthole of his cabin at the forward end of the superstructure. When he called the Chief Mate, John Saxton, to ask why, he learned what had been happening during the last four hours.

The 4-8 watch had been anything but routine for First Mate Jon Thuesen, a native of California and the only one of the four mates who was married. During his final watch on the *Harrison*

50

the ship was transformed from a dignified American passenger ship plying the East China Sea to a defenseless naval auxiliary, desperately trying to retreat from an enemy with overwhelmingly superior forces.

Below in the engine spaces the watchstanders were slowly becoming aware of what was happening topside. At the time that 55-year-old John Griffin, the Third Assistant Engineer, came off watch at four in the morning, the black gang had not yet heard the news of the Pearl Harbor attack. Split into two groups, five in the engine room and three in the separate fireroom, the engine department watchstanders would have not heard the news at the same time. But during the 4-8 watch of the 48-year-old Second Assistant, John Vanderveer from New Jersey, the word reached everyone aboard. When fireman Gil Monreal called the upcoming watch and brought back a status report on what was going on, several of the unlicensed personnel in the fireroom left their posts and went immediately to the lifeboats, suitcases in hand.

In the dim light of dawn the deck gang, under orders from the captain, had begun painting the smokestack of the ship to cover the APL marks with a coat of grey. Other seamen began painting out the American flag on the hull. The work was soon stopped, however, when a Japanese plane appeared overhead firing flares, some of which landed on deck.

With daybreak had come detection. Captain Pierson explains what happened next:

> *Being able to make about 15.5 knots, we had not made many miles when daylight came, and, with it, a Japanese plane with her bomb racks full. She signalled us to stop with a burst of machine-gun fire, and then after circling us flew off towards another ship that was coming up on the horizon. This ship turned out to be the **Nagasaki Maru**, a fast 22-knot mail boat on the Japan-China run. Apparently he had been told to tail us and keep us under surveillance while he reported our whereabouts to the naval authorities in Shanghai. I knew the ship well and realized the futility of trying to escape from her. We were in no way afraid of her, and as soon as we recognized her we got underway, but try as we could we could not lose her. As often as we*

51

*changed course she did the same, and stayed on our
heels. I thought at one time of ramming her, but she
was smart enough to keep well clear of us while still
keeping guard over us.*

This unlikely nemesis, the 5,400-ton *Nagasaki Maru*, was a
small two-stacked passenger ship of the NYK Line. Built in
England in 1921 as a cross-channel steamer, she had instead
spent virtually her entire career as a Japanese ship.

Now that escape no longer seemed possible with both
aircraft and the ship dogging every move of the *Harrison*, it
became necessary to look for another course of action. Captain
Pierson assembled all his officers and reviewed the options. One
option was rejected at the outset: surrendering the vessel
intact. Aware that the ship, undamaged and operational, could
immediately be utilized by the Japanese as a transport, Captain
Pierson was determined not to allow that to happen.

Preventing the ship from falling into Japanese hands in a
usable condition now became his primary concern, along with
the safety of the crew. Scuttling, in the ordinary sense of sinking
the ship, would have been difficult and slow. Although she had
been built as a military vessel, the *Harrison* had no scuttling
valves or system *per se*; neither were there any demolition
explosives aboard. Flooding the engine room through the sea
chest would not have provided enough negative buoyancy since
she was at least a two-compartment ship. With no cargo aboard,
the ship had enormous reserve buoyancy. Any attempt to fill her
holds by gravitating water through the bilge lines or pumping
through fire lines would have taken so long that the Japanese
could have readily recognized what was going on and then
intervened.

Consequently, trying to sink the ship was ruled out as
unworkable. The only remaining possibility was to damage the
ship as severely as possible. Using a chart of the rocky island-
strewn coast of China, the captain pointed to the large number
of wrecks depicted by the standard chart symbol, and observed
that few of the vessels grounding in the area were ever refloated:

*My plan, to which they all agreed, was to run for
the beach and send the ship up as high as possible at
full speed hoping to accomplish this before any further*

52

*ships made their appearance. We had nothing to worry about as far as the **Nagasaki Maru** was concerned (other than her following us), as she was unarmed. We started in the direction of Shaweishan as this was the nearest land...*

In the absence of a logbook or personal diaries with direct notations of time, it is necessary to reconstruct the timetable for the rest of December 8th from general recollections of the captain and several crewmembers. Survivors' accounts differ significantly on important details of the events of this day, so the exact way that these events happened may never be fully reconstructed.

The game of chase with the *Nagasaki Maru* lasted throughout the morning watch of Fourth Assistant Engineer Frank Knowles, at 23 the youngest of the engine officers, and that of Third Mate Sydney Olsen, at 24 the youngest of the deck officers. Olsen, who had been aboard the *Harrison* for almost a year and a half, including his initial trip on which he sailed as an able-bodied seaman, was the son of a prominent West Coast shipmaster, Lars Olsen, who had once been decorated for rescuing 25 people from the steamer *San Benito* in 1896.

Since the ship had run for at least three and a half hours to the southeast and had apparently worked her way back to the west during Olsen's morning watch while trying to evade the *Nagasaki Maru*, it must have been at least mid-day before the *Harrison* was anywhere near her original trackline. The captain's statement that Shaweishan was the nearest land suggests that the ship had also worked her way north; otherwise, the various islands of The Saddles group would have been closer. Thus it was early afternoon before the ship was in position to start the run for Shaweishan Island.

Shaweishan was a small rocky island on the north side of the northerly approach to the mouth of the Yangtze River, normally passed on the starboard hand by ships bound for Shanghai from the north or east. It was almost 200 feet high, somewhat wooded, and crowned by a lighthouse with a 55-foot tower. It also housed a radio beacon.

As the *Harrison* began her approach, a Japanese destroyer began moving toward her at high speed, and the plane reappeared overhead. It now became a race to see if the ship could be put aground before she was intercepted. Code books and classified material were dumped overboard as the ship moved toward the shallow water around the island.

On watch on the bridge was Second Mate Matthew Sullivan, a 32-year-old native of New York state who was the only ship's officer who listed no next of kin on the official crew list. At the helm was the 52-year-old quartermaster, Joseph Pierpoint.

Down below, the longtime Chief Engineer, Joseph C. "Shaky" Smith, and his staff coaxed every revolution they could from the 20-year-old reciprocating engines. Five minutes before the estimated time of the crash they were ordered out of the engine room.

The entire crew of the *Harrison* had been kept informed through the public address system as to what was happening. Extra provisions and blankets had been put into all the lifeboats, and crewmembers stood by at lifeboat stations wearing lifejackets. The lifeboats were swung out. Captain Pierson had planned to hit the steep rounded north side of the island on the port bow, so the impact would rip a long gash in that side of the vessel, opening several compartments to the sea. At the final moment the word "Hang on to the rail" was passed to the crew on deck.

Shortly after one o'clock, making 16 knots, the *President Harrison* plowed into the island, striking first at about the location of number one hold. As Ed Wise recalled the impact, "The disintegration of the ship was deafening, and the motion reminded me of a dog shaking a rat. When we picked ourselves up we were still moving, but soon settled about a thousand feet from the island with our bow resting on the ocean floor and the stern riding high." Other crewmembers had different reactions. Clara Main, the stewardess, remembered a grinding, screeching noise. James Agnew, an ordinary seaman, recalled the grounding as "quite smooth." He remembers the ship sliding up on the shoal and coming to a gradual stop, but with a severe list.

After grinding along the edge of the island the ship listed heavily as she rolled off her contact with the bottom and slid into deeper water. With her screws still turning the ship had enough way on her to move out of shallow water. Not yet sure what he had been able to accomplish, the captain now had to think primarily of the safety of his crew. He recalled,

54

Although unarmed, the *Nagasaki Maru* proved to be a formidable opponent for the *President Harrison*. (Steamship Historical Society of America)

Shaweishan Island was an unlikely place to terminate a voyage of a passenger ship. (John Hallinan)

The lighthouse on Shaweishan Island was the first place in China to house the crew of the *Harrison*. (Howard Allred)

The only woman in the *Harrison* crew, British-born stewardess Clara Main, helped row to the island. (Howard Allred)

The crewmembers of the *Harrison* were understandably curious about their fate while being detained at Shaweishan. (John Hallinan)

*Not knowing exactly how much damage we had
done and whether or not a boiler explosion would
shortly occur, I deemed it advisable to get the crew off
the ship into the boats. As there were no men in the
engine spaces, we shut the steam off by use of the boiler
stops on the boat deck, and shortly thereafter sent the
boats away, except for my own, with orders to make for
the island. We had kept our radio silent until close in;
then I gave the operator orders to open up and get a
message away as to what we were doing. This message
was received and acknowledged, I believe, by a San
Francisco shore station. As the boats were getting away
I went back to the radio shack, and we kept the set
going until the power finally died and we had to quit
for the lack of power to transmit any further. By now
the plane had opened up with his machine-gun and
was strafing the ship, presumably to stop us from using
the radio.*

In charge of the launching of the lifeboats was the Chief
Mate, 41-year-old John Saxton whose career on merchant and
naval vessels spanned 26 years including service on a number of
Dollar Line vessels. Along with Captain Pierson, Saxon was a
Naval Reserve officer. Now he supervised the lowering of boats
into the water as the crew began the depressing task of abandoning the *Harrison*. Abandoning ship was a process which had
been practiced weekly over the life of the ship, but only
occasionally to the full extent of lowering boats into the water
and rowing them or running their engines.

Judging from contemporary pictures, it appeared that the
Harrison had eight boats. Fortunately, none of them was
"nested" or placed in pairs, one on top of another. This
practice, common on passenger ships with many boats, saved
space, but it made the job of launching the lower boat in each
set rather slow since, after launching the upper boat, the
travelling block on the davit boat falls had to be hauled back up
to pick up the second boat out of the chocks before that boat
could be swung out and lowered. These traveling blocks on the
boat falls were not heavy enough to move easily under a light
strain, and therefore tended to topple or to twist the falls. Thus
the second boat generally required somewhat more time to be

launched than did the upper boat. Without this cumbersome second set of boats the *Harrison* was able to launch boats more quickly than could most passenger ships.

Ideally, a deck officer should command each of a ship's lifeboats, but on passenger ships of that era there were more boats than there were deck officers: eight to five in the case of the *Harrison*. The other boats without mates were the responsibilty of senior unlicensed deck personnel such as the bos'n, carpenter, quartermasters, and able bodied seamen, all of whom were qualified lifeboatmen, a credential issued by the Coast Guard. Such boats were assigned other officers, generally engineers, for purposes of internal discipline, but the responsibility for launching the boats and directing their progress underway fell to the lifeboatmen in charge.

There is disagreement among survivors concerning the number of boats that were actually launched from the *Harrison*. Inasmuch as the boats were large enough for 50 people, it is evident that not all boats were needed for the 165 people aboard. Also, the pronounced list and the down-by-the-head angle of the hull may have made it difficult to launch all boats on both sides. However, Alfred Rye, the ship's electrician, remembers going into the last boat on the port side while the chief engineer went into the last boat on the starboard side, so in spite of the awkward angle of the hull the boats on each side were apparently all usable. Captain Pierson recalled later that not all the boats were used, however; upon returning to the ship after the grounding he ordered some remaining lifeboats launched and cut adrift.

In any case, all the lifeboats that were utilized were launched successfully, but one encountered difficulty and drifted toward the port screw which was still turning because of unexhausted steam left in the engine. With the ship now down by the head and listing markedly to starboard, this screw was slicing its way half out of the water. The crew of the lifeboat became panicky and lost control as the boat was drawn into the screw. Men jumped into the water; bodies were tossed into the air as the boat was chewed up by the propeller. Three men lost their lives: Arnold Carlson, a 24-year-old oiler from Portland, Oregon; Francis McGoldrick, a 46-year-old waiter, a naturalized American citizen from England; and Nathan Berman, a 28-year-old bellboy, a native of Russia not yet fully naturalized.

Among the survivors of this ill-fated boat who were picked up by other boats from the oil-smeared and blood-stained water were the 40-year-old Chief Engineer Joseph C. Smith, the third radio officer, 24-year-old Jasper Treadway, Richard Burnside, a 22-year-old pantryman, and the Chief Steward John McKay. The 49-year-old McKay, who had come to the *Harrison* with Captain Pierson when the *President Taft* was sold to the Army, was the only seriously injured victim of the accident. He suffered several broken ribs, and required assistance in getting ashore. Albert Alsop, a 41-year-old room steward from England, was tossed by the screw but received only lacerations.

As the remaining boats of the *Harrison* were rowed away through a sea running with a swift ebb tide they were watched from a safe distance by the Japanese naval commander in the destroyer which was maneuvering to anchor. Eventually the boats were beached in mid-afternoon in a small cove on the island after a vigorous half-mile row from the ship. A long flight of stairs zig-zagged up the steep bluff to the lighthouse above. These stairs were a challenge for some of the crewmembers who were tipsy from having raided the ship's liquor cabinet on their way to the boats. At the lighthouse the Chinese keepers displayed no hostility to the shipwrecked mariners.

As the captain prepared to leave the ship in the last boat there was a momentary hesitation. The ship was not sinking very rapidly and the water was not very deep; perhaps the ship should not be fully abandoned. But the menacing aircraft sporadically raking the bridge with machine-gun fire pointed up the danger of remaining.

While waiting for the Captain two members of the boat crew, ordinary seaman Henry Behrens and oiler Clement Chun, on their own initiative cut loose and cast overboard some of the life rafts. Now, as the captain started down the jacob's ladder, Behrens was uneasy about the prospect of leaving any injured survivors in the water. He thought he saw what could have been a man bobbing in the water near one of the rafts. But the weather had become overcast and foggy, and he could not be sure. When the captain was aboard the boat shoved off under the command of First Mate Jon Thuesen. Although it was a powered boat, the engines chose not to work that afternoon, and the crew, which included the stewardess Clara Main, had to row to the island.

By the time the captain landed on Shaweishan in the last
boat he found that the lighthouse keepers had turned over one
of the small buildings to his crew, and that a meal was being
prepared.   Under the circumstances, both captain and crew
could be grateful that so far they had survived the dangers
inherent in a deliberate and destructive stranding with only a
minimum of discomfort.

Captain Pierson described what happened next:

> *Just as dark came on, which is early at this time of
> the year in these parts, a Japanese Naval Landing Unit
> (which is the same as our Marines) from the destroyer
> landed on the island and made their way to the top,
> bristling with guns and bayonets fixed. I do not know
> what they expected to find but as we had done all we
> could, however good or bad it was, there was nothing left
> to do but get rid of our guns (we threw the few revol-
> vers we had into the bushes) and surrender. First they
> destroyed the lighthouse radio station and then lined
> us all up and searched us for weapons--we had none--
> but anything we had such as money or papers were
> thrown on the ground and left. The entire crew were
> then placed under guard on the island and I was taken
> off to the destroyer where I spent the night.*

Thus began one of the longest and strangest dramas of captivity to emerge from World War II. It opened with rain falling
steadily during the night on the metal roof of the lighthouse at
Shaweishan, creating a din that added to the difficulty for 163
frightened people trying to sleep, under guard, as best they
could. Most were in the large main room, but others slept on
the circular stairway to the light and even in another small
building higher up on the hill. Uncertainty over what would
happen to them next at the hands of their Japanese captors
contributed to anxiety and sleeplessness during the long night
for the crew of the *Harrison*.

Curiously, however, Captain Pierson was being treated with
considerable respect and camaraderie aboard the destroyer, and
even had a reasonably good night. As he recalls,

> *I was taken into the wardroom where I found the*

officers in a jubilant mood with the radio going full blast and, as I soon learned, reports coming of the sinking of the Prince of Wales, the various ships in Pearl Harbor, etc. Of course, the radio was in Japanese, but several of the officers spoke excellent English and they certainly laid it on. They treated me very kindly, however, and later the Commander made his appearance. After telling me how easy it would be for Japan to lick the world, he broke out a bottle of Johnnie Walker Black Label and treated everybody in the wardroom including myself. Later I was given coffee and rice cakes, a bed was made up for me on one of the settees, and I was made as comfortable as possible.

At seven o'clock in the half-dawn of December 9th, 1941, Captain Pierson was brought up on deck of the destroyer and told that he would be returned to the island. A boat from the destroyer started for shore with the captain and a Japanese officer, but was recalled when halfway across by a signal from the ship. After returning to the destroyer the officer went on board briefly and then re-entered the boat, no longer courteous and amicable. Something had happened aboard the destroyer, changing the attitude of the officers towards their American captive. Perhaps seeing for the first time that the ship was aground, her bow on the bottom, and listing heavily to starboard, they realized that the *Harrison* was not the easy prize they had assumed her to be. From that point on, the Japanese became curt and abusive in their dealings with Captain Pierson.

The boat went on to the island where the officer ordered the entire crew back into the beached lifeboats with the exception of the stewardess and the injured chief steward who were left at the lighthouse. As the Japanese Marines lined up the crew on the beach they seemed confused by the ethnic diversity of these Americans they had captured, particularly the Asians and Blacks. They were heard to mutter, *"Wakaranai"* which means "I don't understand."

The weary crew entered the boats again, and started back out to the ship to learn more about their fate. Passenger ship lifeboats are big and bulky, designed with considerable freeboard and buoyancy to float high in the water, but they are not easy to row. They are intended to be mobile enough to get safely away from a sinking ship, but they are not designed as work boats or ferry boats. So the task of getting the *Harrison*'s boats ready for further use, working them off the beach, and covering the half mile back to the ship under oars was strenuous activity for the crew, 74 of whom were at least 40 years of age.

On arrival back at the ship the crew had a difficult time reboarding because of the severe list. Moving about on deck required hanging onto the rails. After the uncomfortable night of fearful anticipation at the lighthouse and the exertion of the long row back to the ship, many of the crew were on the ragged edge. The tension on board was compounded by Japanese sentries, bayonets fixed, standing guard. Passenger agent Wise recalled at least one crew member passing out and others vomiting. Facing the uncertainties of captivity on a crippled ship was understandably a moment of terror for these civilian mariners who had not been trained to handle military confrontations.

A Japanese sailor displayed an American flag over his arm, apparently the ship's ensign which had been flying at the gaff when the ship was abandoned. Now the Japanese naval flag fluttered on the same halyard.

Eventually, the crewmembers were allowed to disperse to their quarters, and the moment of terror passed. After inspecting the damage as best they could, the Japanese officers returned to the destroyer with their three riflemen. For the next few days the Japanese would make ineffective efforts at recovering their lost prize, and the crew of the *Harrison* would begin to settle into this strange new environment as prisoners.

Chapter 5

The Salvage of the *President Harrison*

Before the members of the crew of the *Harrison* were to learn the nature of their long-term confinement by the Japanese they were forced to assist in the salvage of the ship.

The salvage and refloating of ships is probably the most difficult yet gratifying task the naval and maritime establishment is called upon to perform on units of its fleet. Although measurement and computation play their part, much of the salvage work is the product of trial and error, a kind of "seat of the pants" pragmatism. Salvage is a world for practitioners, not theoreticians.

The principles of salvage are the basic concepts of elementary physics--moments of force, fundamentals of hydraulics, simple machines, *et al*--as required by individual cases. A high degree of seamanship is essential. There is, however, an assumption underlying any salvage project, regardless of the techniques required: that all personnel working on the project are pulling together, dedicated to the successful completion of the task. In the case of the *President Harrison*, in which members of the crew participated in the salvage work, that circumstance, as we shall see, did not always prevail.

Nevertheless, in spite of a singular lack of enthusiasm and cooperation on the part of the *Harrison*'s crew, the job turned out better than most of the other salvage jobs the Japanese were to acquire within the next few months as additional American naval and merchant ships were damaged or scuttled.

Seven such American ships are known to have been salvaged by the Japanese for their own use during the first part of the war: five naval vessels, one Army vessel, and one other merchant ship in addition to the *Harrison*. The Yangtze River gunboat *Luzon*, which had carried Admiral Glassford out of Shanghai just hours after the *Harrison* had left, would be scuttled off Corregidor in April of 1942, to be raised and put into service as a Japanese vessel by August of that year. Also sunk at about the same time and place were the damaged minesweeper *Finch* which required a year's work before being ready to serve in the Imperial Navy, and the scuttled fleet tug *Genesee* whose salvage and repair took two years. The Army mineplanter *Colonel George F. E. Harrison*, damaged and sunk in an air raid at Corregidor in April of 1942, joined the Japanese Navy in October of that year.

Elsewhere, in Guam the sunken Navy tanker *Robert L. Barnes* was raised and made fully operational as a ship, a status beyond that she had known in her recent duty as a station ship. In two drydock scuttlings, the destroyer *Stewart* in Sourabaya was ready for service as a Japanese vessel in 14 months, and the freighter *Admiral Y. S. Williams* went back to work as a merchant ship within a few months after her demise in Hong Kong, only to be sunk by an American submarine and salvaged again in Southeast Asia later in the war.

In the case of the scuttled Navy ships, the sinkings were carried out systematically inasmuch as a Scuttle Ship Bill existed on those vessels as a drill to be conducted occasionally; also, scuttling valves and systems were built into the vessels, and explosives were generally available. Merchant crews are not trained in this procedure and their ships normally do not have scuttling systems or carry explosives on board. Thus, the reasonably successful scuttling of the *President Harrison* has to be considered a job well done. By the same token, as the first of the salvage jobs carried out by the Japanese on this group of scuttled and sunken American ships, the one involving the largest ship, and the one whose progress was retarded, even sabotaged at times, the salvage of the *President Harrison* must be regarded as a remarkable accomplishment.

Initial salvage efforts were undertaken quickly by the officers of the Japanese destroyer. Their inspection of the *Harrison* showed that the ship had condsiderable water in the forward holds. Number one was only partially flooded, but two and three had water as high as the upper tweendecks. Number four, a shallow hold under the midships house, also had water to the upper tweendecks, but number five, a similar hold was only partially flooded. The engine room had 12 feet of water, but the after holds were completely dry. The bow was resting on the bottom, but the stern floated free. A pronounced starboard list still existed.

The first order of business was bringing the dead ship back

to life. Before any heat could be put into the cold ship and before electricity could be restored to provide lighting and the instrumentation and control necessary in the engine room, fires under the boilers had to be relighted and pumps restarted. These pumps were necessary to supply drinking water, flushing water, fuel oil, bilge suction, fire mains, and a host of other functions necessary to make the ship operational again.

Gilbert Monreal, who was a 19-year-old fireman on the 4-8 watch, recalls how the engine room was rehabilitated and put back into service:

Not long after arriving aboard, the chief engineer, Mr. Smith, informed us that the Jap officer in charge prodded him in the buttocks with a bayonet and told him if he didn't have steam up on a boiler at 100 pounds in four hours he would be shot. The crew was told to bring anything that would burn to the fire- room. We had to feed a dead boiler, so steam could be raised enough to heat the oil and start the oil service pump. I have a vivid recollection of an armed Jap Marine who spoke no English arriving about every half hour, snarlingly pointing to the steam gauge and pointing to his watch. With good luck, the boiler had not been damaged and we overcame that hurdle.

Next came the engine room. It was partly sub- merged with sea water, due to the ruptured port side of the ship. The engine room was first isolated from the rupture by dropping the watertight doors. It was then that the chief asked me, being the youngest of the crew, to dive down in about eight feet of water to locate and close the suction valve to the condenser and open the bilge suction so the engine room could be pumped dry when enough pressure from the boilers could be gener- ated.

I remember the fellow assisting me was an older man... After several dives I got tired and [he] went down but he couldn't hack it too well, and I finally finished. I don't remember being so cold. The chief thanked us and, after we cleaned up, gave us a bottle of scotch to help warm us up again. ... To this day I admire the chief for his ability and direction in bring-

*ing this dead plant alive in so short a time. Perhaps
he had no choice.*

With the ship again habitable and operable, albeit in a
limited way, a first real try at getting her out of the grasp of the
mud could now be made. After oil and water were transferred
from tank to tank to mitigate the list, the *Harrison* was ready
for whatever procedures her captors might want to try.

Without much attention to the consequences, the Japanese
first tried to pull the ship free with wire ropes from the destroyer. When the standard-size cables parted, the would-be salvors
requisitioned the "insurance cable" from the *Harrison*, a heavy-
duty wire hawser kept on a reel on the stern of merchant ships
for emergency purposes. Even with this cable the destroyer was
unable to budge the half-sunken liner.

It was just as well for the Japanese that the *Harrison* could
not be moved at this point. With five holds open to the sea,
and water in the engine room which had probably gravitated in
through open piping systems, it seems certain that the entire
ship would have sunk if she had been moved to deeper water.
After such a move, even though the ship would have rested on
the bottom, the superstructure would have remained above
water because of the relatively shallow water surrounding the
island. Nevertheless, in this position with decks awash the ship
would have presented a much more difficult salvage job than she
was with her stern still floating high.

Several days were spent on these ineffective efforts to free
the ship. A tug, the *Merry Moller* which only two weeks earlier
had ferried Marines out to the ship in Shanghai, was sent out to
assist, but the *Harrison* did not budge.

Even using the ship's engines along with the pull of the
destroyer and tugboat on the hawser, the *Harrison* still did not
move. She was simply too full of water and too heavily a-
ground. At this point Captain Pierson saw the opportunity to
retard the long-range rehabilitation of the ship. In the guise of
lightening the vessel, he convinced the Japanese that much
equipment should be thrown over the side. The somewhat
gullible Japanese agreed, and considerable equipment, some
peripheral but some important, was dumped overboard. This
material included some motion picture projectors, pianos,
furniture, stores, tarpaulins, hatch covers, and even hatch beams

The *Harrison*, missing her hatch boards, was stripped of useful equipment before the Japanese wised up. (John Hallinan)

The Japanese wasted no time in hoisting the Rising Sun flag at the gaff of their new prize. (John Hallinan)

Alongside to assist in the salvage work is the *Merry Moller* which had brought American Marines to the ship only a few weeks earlier. (John Hallinan)

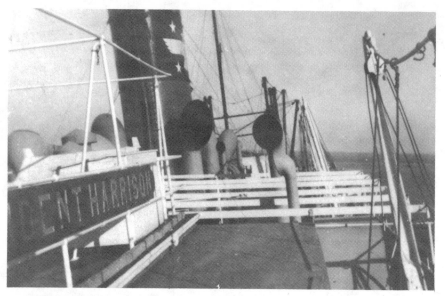

The starboard list of the ship during her salvage is evident in this picture from the flying bridge. (John Hallinan)

This weathered newspaper clipping which survived three and a half years of internment shows how the *Harrison* looked entering Shanghai. (Howard Allred)

CAPTURED U.S. LINER BROUGHT TO SHANGHAI

The American President Line's crack trans- ... aged by a Japanese salvaging vessel on ... Pacific liner President Harrison, 13,000 tons, which ... ing of January 8. Photograph shows the ... beached after having been chased by the Japanese ... Harrison with the Japanese naval ensign ... liner Nagasaki Maru, on December 8, 1941, was re- ... (Press Union) and strongbacks. It was only when the captain suggested that the next step should be the unshipping and sinking of the cargo booms that the Japanese finally drew the line. In the meantime, much equipment that would ultimately have to be replaced had been dumped into the sea; the captain later estimated that $100,000 worth of gear had been jettisoned.

For all practical purposes, the ship was no closer to floating free as a result of this effort. The "tons per inch immersion" factor for the 502 class ships was probably in the range of 55-60, which meant that 55 to 60 tons of weight would have to be removed to lessen the draft by one inch. It is likely that no more than 100 tons of equipment had been discarded, so the net effect of all this activity was minimal.

During this time a pompous Japanese military official, described as an admiral in some accounts, was in charge of the futile salvage efforts. With limited English he exhorted the *Harrison*'s crew: "You get ship Shanghai you very warm; you no get ship Shanghai you very cold." This man was neither popular with the ship's crew, nor effective as a supervisor of salvage.

Finally the Japanese realized that they needed professional salvors. They sent for the Nippon Salvage Company which arrived on the scene shortly with an experienced salvage master and a number of hard-hat divers. Within a few days a proper survey of the vessel had been made, and a plan developed for the salvage job. Long narrow gashes were found along the turn of the bilge on the port side, extending from the number one to number five hold which was virtually amidships. The engine room, although still partially flooded through its piping systems, was not open to the sea. Additional buoyancy was now achieved by pumping the engine room dry, and the list was further mitigated by transferring fuel and water in tanks. Now the serious work of a patch-and-pump salvage job could begin.

After divers had measured the holes in the hull, long wooden patches were fabricated from planking and weighted for placing on the outside of the hull, to be held against the ship by tension from inside the hold. Mattresses were used as gasket materials around patches, and for plugging smaller holes. Wooden 4 x 4s were utilized as shoring to hold those patches placed from the inside of the hull, and to reinforce tank tops and transverse bulkheads. Cement was used in awkward locations in the bilges which could not be reached readily with

65

other forms of patches; this cement could either be poured conventionally with wooden cofferdams keeping water away, or could actually be poured underwater.

The crew of the *Harrison* was utilized directly in many ways in assisting the salvage crew: operating hand pumps for divers, rounding up wooden dunnage to be used in fabricating patches, lowering heavy-duty centrifugal salvage pumps into the lower holds, providing access to the number four and five holds through the side ports, etc. The crew was cooperative but not eager in carrying out these projects. During the latter part of December the work went on day and night, but at a pace as leisurely as the crew could make it.

Communication between the crew of the *Harrison* and the salvage crew was not difficult, for several reasons. First the Japanese salvage master, a man named Ichikawa, had grown up in Portland, Oregon, and spoke good English. In one private conversation he told crewmembers that Japan could not win the war because of the great productivity of the United States. A second aid to communications was in the person of Harry Sasaki, a California-born nisei who was a porter on the *Harrison* and who spoke Japanese well enough to be quite useful to Captain Pierson as his interpreter.

But the most natural facilitation of communication came not from language skill, but the mutual respect and camaraderie that developed between the salvage crew and the ship's crew. These were professional seamen working together to defeat a common enemy, the sea, rather than military forces fighting each other for territory. The Marine guards served as a reminder that a state of war existed, but even in prodding their charges to work faster these guards from time to time showed a sense of the same "men against the sea" camaraderie.

The days spent in salvaging the *President Harrison* must have evoked a number of mixed emotions for the crew, particularly for those in the deck and engine departments. These seamen, against all their professional instincts, had participated earlier in the attempt to destroy the vessel that had been their home for many months. Now they were working to restore the ship to operational status, aware that she could soon be ready to carry troops and cargo against American forces, but unaware of what might next happen to them once their services in rehabilitating the ship were no longer needed. With all these things running though their minds, they continued to work hand in hand with the Japanese salvors--as slowly as possible.

While the stately and historic *President Harrison* would never be the same again, some semblance of her former routine had been maintained after her capture, at least for a few weeks. For Christmas dinner, 1941, a traditional holiday meal was prepared by chief cook Gerald Morgan, consisting of a number of tasty dishes. An attractive menu was run off by the ship's printer, Arthur Norwood, "dedicated to the officers and crew of the S.S. *President Harrison*, shipwrecked at Shaweishan Island, December 8, 1941." On the cover, along with that dedication, were the names of O. A. Pierson, Commander, and "Ribless" McKay, Chief Steward. The latter reference was apparently to the steward's battered ribs, a result of the lifeboat accident.

Inside the menu were listed a dazzling array of four entrees, soup, salads, vegetables, desserts, fruit and cheese, etc. This occasion may well have been the only time in the liner's history that her entire staff was kept busy in grand style serving only each other. In a sense, the meal marked the end of the old established order on the *President Harrison*, and the beginning of a new, yet-to-be-defined way of life.

Under the stress of coping with their new environment and working for the first time against the best interests of the ship, the members of the crew now sometimes put personal interest above the common interests of the group. As prisoners within spaces they knew far better than did their captors, it was easy for crewmembers to rationalize that it was better for them to do a bit of plundering than for the Japanese to do it. Keep it away from the Japanese, seemed to be a useful guideline. Quite understandably, most crewmembers moved into passenger quarters that were better than their own. Raiding and hoarding of food supplies became a problem. The unlicensed members of the deck department even held a session that combined a kangaroo court with a union meeting to deal with officers whom they felt were eating better than they were because of private caches of food. Some of the officers admitted the charge; others denied it.

This incident points up the lack of a back-up system of discipline within the crew of a merchant ship, compared to that which would exist for a military crew. In all fairness, however, it should be noted that military personnel in World War II prison camps commonly displayed the same kind of "look out for number one" attitude that characterized the crew of the *Harrison* at this moment. Nevertheless, this period was certainly not the high point in the behavior of the ship's crew. It perhaps reflected a vacuum of discipline in which the established routine and rules of a merchant ship had been displaced, but not yet replaced by a system of discipline established by the Japanese.

Eventually, with the Japanese taking what they wanted and the *Harrison* crewmembers creating their private caches, food supplies ran low. Fresh water, too, became a problem; showers were prohibited, and crewmembers were reduced to brushing their teeth with such available liquids as Coca Cola. Toward the end of the ship's extended stay at Shaweishan Island some welcome supplies of carrots and cabbages were brought out from Shanghai by the Japanese, along with a water barge. Obviously, things had changed a great deal in the few weeks since Christmas.

The work of patching the hull and pumping out the holds extended into late January 1942. Judging from a pair of pictures of Shaweishan Island taken on different relative bearings from the deck of the *Harrison*, the ship had become lively enough to swing with the tide before she was freed from the sediments of the Yangtze delta. Finally, on the highest tide of the month on the 20th, with a battery of 10-inch pumps straining to discharge water faster than it could enter the ship through leaks around the patches, the *Harrison* came free of the bottom.

In order to trim the ship properly to make her more manageable underway, the previously-dry after holds of the ship were now partially flooded. While this action increased her overall draft, it brought her bow up higher. Although still down by the head, she was now buoyant enough to get underway for Shanghai. As with all large ships, she made the passage on the tide which provided an extra 10 to 12 feet of water over the tricky shoals of the Yangtze and Whangpoo. While the pumps continued to discharge water from the forward holds she limped into Shanghai under her own power, assisted by tugs, still listing to starboard.

Upon arrival the ship was moored at Jardine's wharf in the Hongkew area below Soochow Creek, just astern of the venerable Japanese cruiser *Idzumo*. Flagship of the China fleet, this ship had been built in England in 1899; no longer a first-rate ship of the line, she was largely a training vessel, but she had recently been involved in the destruction of the British gunboat *Peterel* in the Whangpoo.

During the next six weeks the officers and crew of the *Harrison* would stay aboard her, continuing to assist the salvage crew in making the ship as seaworthy as possible while the Japanese authorities decided where to send her next for further repairs.   The Japanese also faced other decisions concerning the ship: which members of the crew were to be imprisoned, and which ones could be set free or repatriated.   Until these decisions were made the seamen of the *Harrison* were all captives of Shanghai. For most of them, that status would be maintained for the next three and a half years.

For the *Harrison* it was now a matter of *deja vu*. In her only other brush with disaster, on the rocks of Bonham Island off the mouth of the Yangtze, she had been damaged enough to require extensive hull repairs in Shanghai before getting underway for the balance of her round-the-world voyage. Now, 15 years later, she was again undergoing major hull repairs--this time caused by her act of self destruction--but there was no schedule to be resumed to the great ports of the world. There was only the prospect of captivity, of serving Japan as a transport in campaigns against the nation whose flag she had displayed so well for so long. That prospect was soon to turn to a reality that would endure for the ship for two and a half years, terminating a year before the end of the war.

The crew of the USS *Wake* became the first group of Americans to be captured during World War II. (U.S. Naval Institute)

Chapter 6

The Officers as Military Captives

Although the crew of the *Harrison* had been captured by sundown of December 8, 1941, those merchant mariners were not the first American prisoners of the new war. That questionable distinction went to the 14-man crew of the USS *Wake*, the gunboat left behind in Shanghai when the Navy and the 4th Marines pulled out in late November. One other group of Americans was also captured earlier than was the crew of the *Harrison*: the embassy and legation guards in North China.

It is not within the scope of this book about the *President Harrison* to describe in any detail the imprisonment of the Shanghai sailors, the North China Marines, or the 4th Marines who were captured later. Other accounts have effectively carried out that responsibility with more authority and detail than any second-hand account could provide. Nevertheless, a brief description of that captivity will be included here for three reasons. First, these were the men whose presence in China was responsible for the *Harrison* becoming entangled in the web of war; ignoring their fate would make the story incomplete and somewhat heartless. Second, and most important, the officers of the *Harrison* were to be imprisoned along with some of these Marines in the same camps for most of the war. Inasmuch as the only surviving *Harrison* officer who has been located during the research for this book has only a dim memory of life in the camps, what we know of the treatment of the ship's officers we know largely through the accounts provided by the military men and other merchant seamen in the Shanghai POW camps. Third, the presence of the Marines in these camps may have contributed significantly to the well-being of the *Harrison* officers and other merchant seamen. For all these reasons we need to know something about this group of prisoners.

This summary of the activities of the military captives will be carried forward in this chapter to its logical and chronological conclusion, making it necessary in succeding chapters to return to 1942 to pick up the rest of the story of the *Harrison* and her crew.

On the 8th of December 1941, the USS *Wake* had been left behind in Shanghai under the command of a lieutenant commander in the Naval Reserve with the memorable name of Columbus Darwin Smith. In civilian life a merchant marine captain and a pilot on the Yangtze and Whangpoo Rivers, Smith had been on active duty for only one week. He was no stranger to active duty, however; as a young ensign in World War I he had won the Navy Cross while commanding a submarine chaser in the battle of Durazzo in the Adriatic Sea. A mariner since he was 16 when he first shipped in schooners in the Gulf of Mexico, he had held his first command in sail at age 20, spent a number of years with the Barber Line and later an equal amount of time with Yangtze Rapid Steamship Company, an American company for whom he had made 122 round trips from Ichang to Chungking on the wild upper Yangtze before settling down into the quieter life of a Shanghai pilot. He was 48 when Admiral Glassford persuaded him to return to active duty to command the *Wake*.

The American gunboat with 10 crewmen aboard was overrun around four in the morning by a boatload of Japanese marines before the single watchstander on deck could sound an alarm or set off the scuttling charges that had been rigged for such an emergency. At about the same time the Japanese were besieging and demanding the surrender of the British gunboat *Peterel* which was moored nearby with a similar skeleton crew of 20, 17 of whom were aboard. Her captain was also aboard, 55-year-old Lieutenant Stephen Polkinghorn, RNR, a former merchant navy captain and river pilot on the Hai Ho at Tientsin.

Lieutenant Commander Smith of the *Wake* was ashore at the time of this pre-dawn confrontation. He was notified by telephone during the assault and came to the Bund but was unable to board his ship. With the scuttling charges still unfired the Japanese captured the *Wake* without resistance, undamaged, and fully operational--the only American vessel so captured in World War II. All members of the crew on board were taken prisoner except a Filipino chief steward who went over the side and swam to the Shanghai side where he was to elude captivity for the balance of the war.

While Smith was on the quay learning the fate of his ship the Japanese were standing by to open fire on the *Peterel* which

Polkinghorn had refused to surrender. After he had been told by the doughty captain to "Get off my bloody ship!" the Japanese boarding officer withdrew to his launch, fired a Very pistol into the air as a signal, and ordered the beginning of the attack on the *Peterel*. Within a few minutes, the gutsy little gunboat, returning fire with only her machine guns against the heavy guns of a destroyer and the cruiser *Idzumo*, was literally blown apart. She sank quickly, aided by her scuttling charges which were set off by the fires raging aboard.

Now began the high drama of Shanghai's only real taste of surface combat during World War II. The survivors of the *Peterel* were forced to swim through the frigid and murky waters of the Whangpoo to reach the Bund. As they did, Japanese marksmen ashore and on the newly-captured *Wake* sniped at them with rifle fire. Then occurred one of the truly unexplained miracles of the war. A fleet of sampans put out from the shore, and, with no real reason to run such a risk, picked up the struggling swimmers and returned to the Bund with these survivors, every one of whom was wounded to some degree. Most of the crewmen were taken aboard the Panamanian-flag freighter *Morazon* by her Norwegian captain and provided with blankets and hot food and drink until the Japanese arrived to take custody of the captives. Eventually they were given medical attention before being taken to the Kiangwan Naval Landing Station where they were imprisoned with the men of the *Wake*.

Six of the 17 crewmen aboard the *Peterel* died. Three men were ashore on leave, two of whom eventually turned themselves in, while the third, radioman Jim Cuming, remained at large throughout the war. The Japanese-controlled Shanghai newspapers soon were high in their praise for the men of the *Peterel* for their courage they displayed during the final hours of the ship.

According to a story appearing in *Colliers* Magazine in July 1942, two crewmen of the *Wake* escaped from captivity during the first few days after the capture of the ship. Sam Logan and a shipmate he knew only as "Bill," overpowered their guards at Kiangwan, escaped through a sewer to Soochow Creek, caught a ride across with a sampan boatman, and, on the Bund, boarded a motorized barge which they took to be Dutch in registry. The officers of this vessel concealed the fugitives in the coal bunkers until they reached the open sea. Several days later the two men were put ashore in a small boat off northern Luzon. Once ashore they luckily found an American unit, largely Marines, pulling out of the area around Olongapo. After this unit had withdrawn to the Manila area the two firemen were assigned to the USS *Peary*, a flush-deck four-stack destroyer of the Asiatic Fleet. This ship soon left for Australia, escaping aerial bombing on several occasions enroute. Finally, in February 1942, she was sunk in the Japanese air raid on Darwin. Sam Logan survived and was returned to the States, but the other fireman died in the attack.

In addition to the men of the *Wake*, another small group of American military personnel was also still in Shanghai: four men of the 4th Marines who had been left behind to close out the accounts and business affairs of the unit. These men, Quartermaster Clerk Paul G. Chandler, First Sergeant Nathan A. Smith, Supply Sergeant Henry Kijak, and Staff Sergeant Loren O. Schneider, were rounded up at the time the crew of the *Wake* was captured; however, as we shall see later, they were eventually assigned a special status as detainees. There may also have been as many as half a dozen stragglers from the *Oahu* and *Luzon* still in Shanghai who had been left behind when the Navy gunboats had hurriedly left. Their fate is unknown.

But the largest number of American military personnel to be detained on December 8th was the group known as the North China Marines, the detachments at Peking, Tientsin, and Chinwangtao which had been awaiting the arrival of the *President Harrison* for their evacuation. Each of these detachments had a somewhat different experience with the Japanese on Pearl Harbor Day, and there was only limited opportunity for communication among the three units at that time.

Camp Holcomb at Chinwangtao was the first to be overrun; as the smallest and most remote post, that outcome was to be expected. Shortly after daybreak the camp was full of Japanese soldiers, shouting and otherwise indicating their presence. Overhead, fighter planes appeared, and offshore a Japanese naval vessel stood by.

It is not clear who was in charge of the Marines in Chinwangtao at this moment. Marine histories indicate that Lieutenant Richard M. Huizenga was in charge of the detachment, but that he was at the docks, three miles away, when the Japanese arrived, leaving his warrant gunner, William A. Lee in charge, and

The Japanese Special Landing Forces enjoyed their first day aboard the captured USS *Wake*. (Naval Historical Center)

This Japanese photograph, taken from the *Idzumo*, shows the attack on the *Peterel*. (Naval Historical Center)

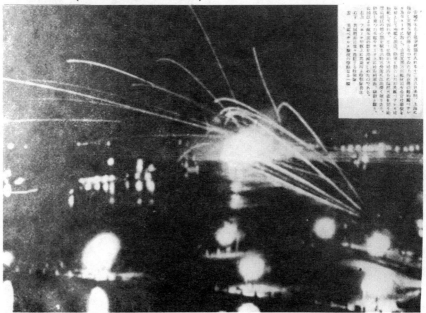

No longer a first-line Japanese cruiser, the *Idzumo* still maintained an intimidating presence in Shanghai. (U.S. Naval Institute)

Columbus D. Smith, captain of the *Wake*, lost his ship to the enemy, but vindicated himself through a remarkable escape from Shanghai. (Naval Historical Center)

Colonel William W. Ashurst visited the Japanese embassy in Peking to surrender his North China Marines. (U.S. Marine Corps)

that he was then summoned back by a messenger. But eye-witness accounts indicated that both Huizenga and Lee had left on a duck hunting trip at six a.m., and returned together to face the Japanese when summoned by a messenger. In their absence Jack Bishop, a platoon sergeant who was the senior non-commissioned officer, reportedly had been directing the preparations.

In any event, the Chinwangtao Marines assumed that they would soon be fighting. They set up defensive positions along the string of boxcars on the nearby railroad tracks, and in the barracks as well where one machine-gun was set up on a pile of footlockers which had been sent from Peking as baggage to go aboard the *Harrison*. One or more of these footlockers may have contained the bones of Peking Man. In addition to machine-guns, Browning automatic rifles, or BARs as they were universally and affectionately known, were also set up, and reportedly even some anti-tank guns were available. No shots were fired, but a lopsided standoff developed.

Huizenga took charge. When a group of four Japanese soldiers approached under protection of a white flag to demand that the unit be surrendered, he ordered the men captured. He then met with a Japanese captain who spoke English; this officer granted Huizenga time to communicate with his superiors in Tientsin. The young lieutenant then radioed Tientsin, "Have set up machine-guns and think we have a chance to stand them off. Request instructions." Major Luther A. Brown, commanding the Tientsin detachment, promptly replied. "Do not--repeat not--resort to fire except in self-defense. Comply with demand of Japanese forces."

Acceding to his instructions from the chain-of-command and the demands of the Japanese, Huizenga surrendered the detachment at 10:40 a.m. The brave but futile effort at defending Camp Holcomb, carried out in the best traditions of the Marine Corps, had come to an end.

The Japanese siege at the Tientsin Marine barracks was characterized by a more formal set of actions than took place during the confrontation at Chinwangtao. While there was no behavior as incongruous as duck hunting, there were, however, moments of irony and even one or two of humor.

Shortly before eight a.m. the executive officer, Captain John A. White, received a telephone call from the Japanese indicating that their Army had taken over the British concession by force, and that Major Omura would soon make a personal call on the Marine unit. An orderly then brought in two urgent radio messages from Washington. One, signed by Secretary of State Cordell Hull, announced the bombing of Pearl Harbor, and the other from Navy secretary Frank Knox, said "Execute WPL 46 against Japan."

When Captain White reported this news to Major Brown, the two officers agreed that WPL must mean *war plan*, but they had no idea what plan 46 was all about. Executing it, in any case, now seemed rather moot under the circumstances. One prior instruction *was* executed, however, as the single-word message "Jabberwocky" was sent to Admiral Hart in Manila, with Colonel Ashurst in Peking as an information addressee. In accordance with the earlier instructions Captain White removed the DITOF code from the safe and burned it in the furnace.

At nine a.m. Major Omura arrived at the head of a 5-man delegation which included an interpreter and a cameraman. He presented a handwritten proposal to Major Brown, calling for the surrender of the Marines in Tientsin and Chinwangtao by one p.m. that day. Omura pressed for an immediate response to the surrender document. Major Brown reminded the Japanese officer that on the previous afternoon the two of them had drunk a toast together with Ranier beer to peace between Japan and the United States. Omura responded through his interpreter that he remembered the moment well, and that he was sorry that circumstances were now different.

Brown then initiated a strategem that was to buy both time and decent treatment for the Marines in the weeks to come. Pointing out that the Marines were stationed in North China under the terms of the Boxer Protocol of 1901, he reminded Omura that signatories to that document--which included Japan and the United States--agreed in case of war to permit repatriation of forces to their respective home countries. Omura seemed impressed; he telephoned his superior, Lieutenant General Kyoji Tominaga, an officer whom the Marines had come to like and respect, and after a brief conversation, announced that the matter would be investigated in Tokyo.

Actually, no such provision existed in the Boxer Protocol. This document, generally regarded as one of the "unequal treaties" imposed upon China, gave the right to foreign nations to station troops in North China. It was this treaty that permitted the Marines to keep 200 fighting men in the area, rather than only a few embassy and legation guards. State Department officials had earlier talked about the existence of a repatriation provision in the Protocol, but this was evidently wishful thinking on their part. The idea of citing the non-existent provision on this occasion came from Lieutenant (junior grade) William Foley, USN, the medical officer, who had suggested it as the Marine officers were discussing their position prior to Omura's arrival.

From all indications, Foley acted in good faith, believing that repatriation was assured by the treaty. The 30-year-old doctor, a native of New York City and a graduate of the Cornell University Medical College, had been in China for three years, serving first as a Navy medical officer in Hong Kong and then in a similar capacity for the North China Marines since May of 1941. In both locations he had established teaching, researching, and practicing arrangements with local Chinese hospitals. He had a wide circle of Chinese friends, spoke Mandarin, and thus was considered as something of a resident China expert among the Marines.

Now the repatriation ploy began to work. The Japanese permitted Major Brown to telephone Colonel Ashurst in Peking; during this conversation the Colonel recommended compliance with all Japanese demands, but he also was noticeably interested in the notion of repatriation. After this call arrangements were made for the actual surrender of the Tientsin detachment. At one p.m. a Japanese lieutenant with 30 soldiers supervised the transfer of all American weapons and ammunition in the basement armory of the compound. Marine officers were allowed to keep their sidearms and one round of ammunition; whether this gesture represented a Japanese invitation to a face-saving suicide can only be a matter of speculation.

Later in the day Lieutenant Huizenga and the Chinwangtao detail arrived to join the parent command in surrender. As John White wrote many years later as a retired colonel,

> *Thus concluded "Pearl Harbor Day" in Tientsin. No shooting, no heroics, nor great drama, only sorrow and frustrations marked the day. A professional military officer, a Marine, I prepared 10 years to defend the United States. Such preparations now proved futile.*

Although the detachment in Peking had twice as many men as did the other two units combined, considerably less has been written about the events of December 8, 1941, at this location than at the other two. Incidentally, the number of men reported at each location varies somewhat from account to account. The numbers cited in the previous chapter (141 at Peking, 49 Tientsin, and 14 at Chinwangtao) are from Colonel White's account. These numbers added to 204, the figures generally cited as the total for the North China Marines. Christopher Janus in writing about Peking Man used 144, 38, and 18, respectively, as the strength of the individual units, for a total of 200. Gerald Beeman, an ex-North China Marine, recalled 144, 38, and 22 as the totals. It is clear that several men were in transit at all times, particularly as couriers and as guards on trains, so the totals could easily vary from time to time for each unit.

Inasmuch as the embassy Marines in Peking were not required to maintain a continuous radio watch on frequencies connecting them to Commander, Asiatic Fleet, in Manila, the first word of the outbreak of war received by Colonel Ashurst was from local Japanese military forces, just as it was for the Marines in Tientsin and Chinwangtao. Apparently even the American embassy learned from the same source that the attack had been made on Pearl Harbor. Ashurst was given until noon to decide whether to fight or surrender, but was allowed to communicate by radio with Admiral Hart in Manila and with Major Brown at Tientsin. There is no indication as to what he was told by Admiral Hart.

The official Marine Corps history of World War II describes what happened next:

> *In a sense Ashurst had been given a Hobson's choice; he could surrender or he could let his troops, fewer than 200 officers and men, be overwhelmed. If discipline and spirit would have won the day, Ashurst could have opened fire on the besiegers--his men had already demonstrated at Camp Holcomb that they were willing to take on hopeless odds. But there was no purpose in fighting if the end result could only be useless bloodshed. In the absence of instructions to the*

78

contrary, Colonel Ashurst took the only sensible course open to him and ordered his men to lay down their arms.

Colonel William W. Ashurst, commanding officer of all Marines in North China, was eminently qualified to lead men into the uncertainties of captivity. A native of Missouri, he was 48 years old at the start of the war. He had put together an outstanding record in the Corps without benefit of either an Annapolis education or a college degree. After being wounded as a lieutenant at Belleau Wood in 1918 and winning the Croix de Guerre and Silver Star for his World War I exploits, he had spent much of his between-the-wars service as one of the Corps' most outstanding marksmen, including winning the national rifle title in 1924. He was commanding officer of the 4th Marines in Shanghai 1930-1933, and later was the top Corps expert in marksmanship, earning the responsibility for testing the new Garand carbine prior to the war. He had commanded the North China Marines since June of 1941.

Now, as December 8th came to an end on the China coast, Colonel Ashurst found himself in an unenviable position, as he joined the company of two other American officers who, during the long day, had seen their commands overrun by the Japanese: Lieutenant Commander Columbus D. Smith of the USS *Wake* and Captain Orel A. Pierson of the SS *President Harrison*.

In the United States the news of Pearl Harbor momentarily pushed everything else aside, including other war news, but within a couple of days the events in China were reported. Considering the enormous volume of follow-up materials moving on the wires relative to the start of the war, the news services did a reasonably good job of picking up the story of the capture of the *Harrison*. One San Francisco paper on December 8th, citing sources in Manila, had some of the facts right and others wrong. It reported that the *Harrison* had been "either seized or sunk" in the Yangtze River, but it went on to describe the non-existent sinking of the transport *Hugh L. Scott* in the Pacific. This is a curious mistake, because some months later a wire service caption on a picture of the captured *Harrison* said, in quoting the original Japanese caption, that "the vessel ... had been renamed *Gen. Hugh L. Scott*." Remember that the Shanghai newspaper in November 1941, had speculated about the ship to be used in evacuating the Marines in such a way as to suggest that the *Hugh L. Scott*, ex-*President Pierce*, was that ship. The mystery is heightened by the fact that on December 8th, 1942, Domei, the official Japanese news agency, in a "one-year-ago-today" story recalled the sinking of the *Hugh L. Scott* off Manila in 1941. The *Scott*, of course, was not involved in such a sinking at that time and place; she was sunk as a naval transport in the North African landings in November 1942. Furthermore, no American ship was sunk off Manila early in December of 1941. The Japanese confusion on this point is inexplicable.

The San Francisco *Chronicle* on December 10th ran an Associated Press story about the *Harrison* datelined Tokyo, December 9th, attributed to Domei. A second story in the *Chronicle* the same day, quoting a German radio station in Shanghai monitored by Associated Press, even had accurate details of the capture of the ship, and a list of her officers. The *New York Times* on the same day ran a picture of the *Harrison* with a caption briefly mentioning her capture, but no story. Thus, certain newspapers with a maritime orientation reported the capture of the ship, but national coverage of the event appears to have been rather limited.

Weekly news magazines, in assessing the total impact of the Japanese attacks on Pearl Harbor and at various locations in the Far East immediately thereafter, acknowledged the capture of the North China Marines as well as the small cadre in Shanghai, but made no mention of the capture of the *Harrison* and her crew. The American President Lines was prohibited from commenting on the loss of the ship. Furthermore, neither the Navy Department nor the Maritime Commission seem to have announced the loss of the *Harrison* and several other merchant ships which had been sunk during the first few days of the war. Consequently, the general public in the United States by reading *Time*, *Life*, or *Newsweek* knew of the capture of some American servicemen in China, but knew nothing about any merchant seamen.

After the surrender of the North China Marines on Pearl Harbor Day the embassy guards in Peking remained in their quarters for the next three weeks under a loose form of house arrest. Similar conditions prevailed at Tientsin where life in the Marine barracks took on a remarkable degree of normalcy, considering that the men were all prisoners. Military instruction continued, and even rifle marksmanship practice was permitted.

The North China Marines in captivity were housed first at the Marine Compound in Tientsin. (U.S. Marine Corps)

Marching between railroad stations in Nanking, the North China Marines were on their way to prison near Shanghai. (Colonel Luther A. Brown)

Among those imprisoned initially at Kiangwan were (l to r) CDR Woolley, LCDR Smith, LT Polkinghorn, and quartermaster Chandler. (Peter Oldham)

Camp leaders at Woosung conferred with their Japanese captors. (l to r) COL Ashurst, CDR Thyson, MAJ Brown, MAJ Devereux, CAPT White, merchant captain MacKinnon, Dr. Kahn, merchant captain Peters, civilian engineer Rutledge, and medical corpsmen. (*Freedom*, Japanese propaganda publication)

The available stocks of low-cost, high-quality liquor were consumed in the barracks during long talks into the night in which the hostilities were regarded by the Marines as a fairly "decent" war, after all. In early January the Peking Marines were brought to Tientsin and housed in the same barracks. Their enthusiasm over the prospect of repatriation, plus their own ample stock of liquor, prompted reunion get-togethers in the barracks, with the prevailing mood that of short-timers.

With the false hope of repatriation in their minds, only a few Marines tried to escape from this relatively informal captivity. Two men hid in the tower of the barracks for three days, but eventually turned themselves in when they could no longer endure the freezing weather without heat.

Once the United States had established diplomatic contact with the Japanese through the Swiss government, the status of the North China Marines could be addressed. In a telegram on December 23, 1941, relative to repatriation the Swiss government was requested to inform Japan that "The United States Government considers that its official personnel subject to this exchange includes ... the Marine guards remaining in China and there under the protection of international agreement..."

The Japanese government replied that "It is unable to agree to include United States Marine Guards remaining in China as they constitute a military unit." The State Department, anxious to see that some kind of repatriation program be undertaken for the large number of Americans in China, did not press the issue of the Marines any further for the moment. Japan inferred from this position that the United States had given up its insistence that the Marines be included in any exchange of diplomatic personnel. The opportunity was lost; soon thereafter, when repatriation was no longer a possibility for the North China Marines, the Leathernecks learned that their British Marine counterparts from Peking were going home.

A few isolated repatriations took place as exceptions to the general rule. Major Edwin P. McCauley, a retired Marine living in Peking, had been recalled to active duty to serve as a quartermaster for the Peking detachment. After the outbreak of the war the Japanese quartered him in a hotel in Tientsin before later returning him to the United States on the first exchange ship. Four other Marines, members of the 4th Regiment, were also repatriated; these were the men left behind in Shanghai to close out the business of the unit when the regiment was evacuated by the *Harrison* and *Madison*. For some reason, the Japanese regarded these men as having diplomatic status, and they were allowed to leave China in the summer of 1942 aboard the Italian exchange ship *Conte Verde*. An old China hand and official historian of the Yangtze River Patrol, retired Navy Rear Admiral Kemp Tolley reports that another American officer was repatriated at this time, Lieutenant (junior grade) Al Kilmartin, nominally the executive officer of the *Wake* who was in China as a language student. Interestingly, in his book Columbus D. Smith does not mention having an executive officer.

With the collapse of Japanese-American negotiations on the repatriation of the North China Marines these men now came to the end of their seven-week "phony war." Late in January 1942, they were marched off to the Tientsin railroad station in the middle of the night; there they were loaded into boxcars for the trip to the Shanghai area where they were to be imprisoned. During the two-day trip they were marched through the streets of Nanking while changing railroad stations. A photograph of this march has been widely utilized in later accounts of Marine captives in the war. Apparently taken by Major Brown at some risk to his personal safety, this picture shows a group of well-uniformed but weaponless Marines marching briskly along with their Japanese captors.

The first home for these prisoners in the Shanghai area was at Woosung where the Whangpoo River joins the Yangtze. Here they would eventually meet the officers of the *Harrison*. This camp was a former Japanese Army post of about 20 acres, completely enclosed with two electrified fences. The seven barracks buildings were all single-story frame structures without heat. Even as they entered camp the Marines were assured that they were not prisoners of war, although they would be treated as such until they were repatriated. Thus, the hope of repatriation was kept alive until the exchange ships came and left in mid-1942.

In addition to the approximately 200 men of the North China Marines this camp and its successor would hold the captain and crew of the USS *Wake*, the crew of the *Peterel*, the soon-to-be-repatriated mop-up detail from the 4th Marines, about 400 Marines and 600 civilian construction workers from Wake Island which fell in late December, several officials of British

Empire countries, and later some Italian troops and mariners. The British group included Sir Mark Young who was Governor General of Hong Kong, Stephen Polkinghorn, the New Zealander who had commanded HMS *Peterel* when that vessel was sunk by the Japanese at Shanghai, and Maurice Lynch, a Canadian doctor attached to the Middlesex Regiment at Hong Kong who had survived the sinking of the prison ship *Lisbon Maru*.

American merchant marine personnel were also imprisoned in these camps. But unlike the crew of the *Harrison* which was split up with officers treated as Naval Reservists to be imprisoned and the balance of the crew as civilians to remain at large, the crews of these other merchant ships were kept intact at Woosung. In February the crew of the SS *Malama* arrived; this ship, a Matson Line freighter carrying secret Army aircraft-detection equipment, had been scuttled to prevent her from falling into Japanese hands as two surface raiders tried to capture her in the South Pacific. Arriving at the same time were the survivors from the SS *Vincent*, a freighter of the American Pioneer Line which had been torpedoed by the same surface raiders, the *Hokoku Maru* and the *Aikoku Maru*. In addition, officers from at least one Norwegian and British ship were in the camp, as well as several China coast captains of the Moller and China Steam Navigation Company fleets. For the most part, each group of officers was quartered separately by unit or nationality in its own building or section, but there was some mixing of personnel. Jon Thuesen, first officer of the *Harrison*, roomed with Gilbert Naysmith, the Scottish first officer of the British ship *Ben Nevis*.

At about the time the *Harrison* officers were leaving the ship to enter the series of prison camps, far to the south the Asiatic Fleet was disintegrating as a fighting force. A few ships retreated to Australia, a few small vessels remained at Corregidor for another few weeks, and there were still submarines in the Far East operating under the control of the Submarine Force in Hawaii. But there was no longer an Asiatic Fleet, even in name, so the one command which the Naval Reserve Ship *Harrison* had served was now, like the ship, a casualty of the war.

By using legal depositions dealing with the officers' rights in certain post-war court cases as well as diaries kept by other prisoners it is possible to reconstruct with some accuracy the initial imprisonment of the *Harrison's* licensed personnel. Leaving the ship in March of 1942, they were first detained at the Kiangwan Naval Landing Station on the north side of Shanghai, a much better facility than the Kiangwan Army Prison Camp which they would also occupy in time. On June 3, 1942, they were moved to Woosung where they joined the Marines, civilian construction workers, gunboat crews, and the merchant captains and crews imprisoned there. Also moving from Kiangwan to Woosung at the same time were 11 military officers and men from the British consulate in Shanghai. The group from the *Harrison* apparently consisted of 19 officers: four mates, eight engineers, four pursers, and three radio operators. The ship's doctor, normally considered an officer, was allowed to remain at liberty in Shanghai where he operated a clinic out of the Foreign YMCA.

Captain Pierson was not with his officers. As he described his own fate,

> *I was taken to Japan the first of April, 1942, to attend, as they said, a prize court. I was confined along with quite a few China Coast men in the Sasebo Naval Hall, and until the middle of August no person asked me a single question concerning the* **Harrison** *(Japanese, I mean). And then one day the Court, consisting of one man and his interpreter, made his appearance and asked me a series of routine questions. They informed me that they thought it would go very bad for me for the damage we had caused. At this time I was the only person in the camp except for four Philippinos, and I spent the six longest weeks of my life in virtually solitary confinement, being allowed out of doors only one hour per day. At the end of this time they returned and asked me the same questions over again, apparently to see if they could trip me up. A few days later I was taken under guard and blindfolded (part of the time) to Zentsuji War Prison Camp on the island of Shikoko. This was a military prison, and I was sent there apparently because I held a Lt. Comdr.'s commission in the U.S. Naval Reserve.*
>
> *I arrived at Zentsuji on November 5th, 1942, and remained there until June 23rd, 1945, when the camp was broken up, and we were transferred to Roko Roshi Camp in the mountains of western Honshu. The story*

of my years in prison camps closely parallels that of any American held by the Japanese with all the heartaches, abuses, uncertainties, and slow starvation accorded to them in the military prisons.

The Zentsuji camp in which Captain Pierson spent the bulk of his confinement was essentially an officers' camp which the Japanese regarded as among the best of all their camps. Pierson reported that the Geneva and Hague conventions were generally adhered to at both Zentsuji and Roko Roshi.

Back on the mainland, the prisoners in the two Shanghai POW camps were ultimately brought together into a single group at the Kiangwan Army Prison Camp when, at the end of 1942, the Japanese closed the swampy camp at Woosung because of a malaria epidemic. This outbreak had resulted in a number of Japanese casualties including the camp commander, while none of the under-nourished prisoners died.

As one might expect, there was never enough to eat in these camps. A watery stew was standard fare; Columbus D. Smith calculated that in these meals a pound of meat was stretched to feed 33 men. At Kiangwan the situation improved when the Japanese allowed the prisoners to plant a vegetable garden which provided needed food as well as a creative outlet for the prisoners.

Shanghai's winter climate is generally damp and chilly. Even though the city is farther south than San Diego and Savannah, its temperature is influenced by air masses from central Asia, and cold winds and storms create raw, biting weather at times.

In spite of the lean fare and the cold winters, the Woosung/Kiangwan camps, generally speaking, were probably among the most humane and tolerable of the POW camps operated by the Japanese. Their proximity to Shanghai helped considerably in that the International Red Cross was able to deliver a number of packages, a useful "underground" was established with the local population, and generous benefactors, including an ex-Navy man, a noted restaurateur named Jimmy James, were able to provide recreational material and foodstuffs well beyond any capabilities the Japanese might have possessed, had they been so inclined. Other benefactors included the unlicensed crewmembers of the *Harrison* who were able to send "CARE" packages to their officers from time to time. The British Resident Association and the American Association were both helpful in supporting military POWs as well as civilian internees. The former group, because of its larger size, was particularly effective. Through mid-1943 it was able to provide food with a daily nutritional value of 757 calories to each of the 80 men in the British contingent, a substantial addition to the food supplied by the Japanese.

Strong leadership existed at Woosung/Kiangwan through a number of officers experienced in command. Colonel Ashurst was the senior of these officers; others were Commander W. C. Cunningham and Major James P. S. Devereux from Wake Island, Commander John B. Woolley of the Royal Navy in Shanghai, Lieutenant Commander Smith from the *Wake*, Lieutenant Polkinghorn from the *Peterel*, and two merchant captains, Malcolm R. Peters of the *Malama* and Angus MacKinnon of the *Vincent*, plus the British and Norwegian captains.

In a Japanese-staged display of the enlightened management of the camp, *Life* Magazine on September 14, 1942, showed a number of photographs, including most of this power structure sitting around a conference table with the Japanese camp officials, presumably discussing the welfare of the prisoners. Missing from the picture were Cunningham, Woolley, and Smith who had been imprisoned for an escape attempt; also missing because they were locked up for suspected complicity in the attempt were Polkinghorn and Dr. Foley. The officers of the *Harrison* had not yet arrived in camp at the time these pictures were taken in March 1942.

While there were a number of endemic prison camp health problems to contend with, no less than five doctors were available to care for the 1,400-1,600 prisoners: Dr. Foley from Tientsin; Dr. Leo C. Thyson, the senior Navy medical officer from Peking; Dr. G. Mason Kahn, a Navy doctor from Wake Island; Dr. Maurice Lynch, the Canadian physician from the British Army; and Dr. Eric G. F. Pollard, the Navy dentist from Peking. Even Dr. Shindo, the Japanese camp doctor, was a humane and decent individual who was concerned for the health of the entire camp.

The relative security of life in the Woosung/Kiangwan camps was offset, however, by the presence of a particularly sadistic camp official, Isamu Ishihara, dubbed "The Beast of the East" by all prisoners with whom he came in contact. A onetime

Honolulu taxi driver, Ishihara was actually an interpreter rather than camp commander or guard, but he seemed to exercise far greater control over prisoners than his position warranted. Although he was not directly responsible for the death of any prisoner, his repertoire of brutality included the Oriental water torture which was inflicted on several prisoners, including Dr. Foley. At the end of the war Ishihara, instead of commiting harakiri as he had indicated he would, cut off the tip of his little finger as expiation for Japan's defeat, explaining that since he was not a soldier, only a contract employee of the Army, that limited action was sufficient. Convicted as a war criminal, Ishihara died in prison 11 years after the end of the war.

Escapes from Woosung were attempted from time to time, but none was successful. In March of 1942 five men broke out, including Lieutenant Commander Smith, Commander Cunningham, and Commander Woolley, along with Dan Teeters, senior civilian engineer at Wake Island and Liu, the Chinese cabin boy of the *Wake*. Within a day the entire group was captured. Several months later four Marines escaped from Woosung, and were at liberty for about a week before being caught. Both groups which had attempted escape were transferred to Ward Road jail in Shanghai.

Two years later, Smith, Woolley, and Jerold Story, one of the earlier Marine escapees, successfully escaped from this Shanghai jail and reached Chungking where they were repatriated by air. This escape was remarkable in its own right for the great distances covered through territory still generally under Japanese control, but it was even more so in that Smith was suffering from a double hernia acquired while stretching to cut the bars of his cell before breaking out of jail. At the same time Commander Cunningham led a separate escape group of five men, but this group was quickly recaptured. In 1945 a group of five prisoners including Lieutenant Huizenga dropped off a train carrying them to North China and successfully escaped; two others tried later in the journey, with one man reportedly getting away. All these later attempts were made after prisoners had been moved away from Woosung and Kiangwan; the record of no successful escapes from these camps continued to stand throughout the war.

No accounts of brutality, escape attempts, or any noteworthy prisoner behavior mention any of the officers of the *President*

Harrison. One would have to conclude that these men were quiet, cooperative prisoners, accepting their fate stoically. Perhaps after their experiences at Shaweishan Island they chose not to rock the boat for the balance of the war. Contenting themselves with minor accomplishments, they enriched their bleak lives behind barbed wire with new friends and new experiences.

Even with a median age of 40 and several of their number well into their 50s, the officers of the *Harrison* had no corner on seniority in the camp. Captain Polkinghorn and Sir Mark Young were well into their fifties; Herman G. Raspe, a civilian who headed the work detail for men over 50, was in his sixties. This sexagenarian once bested a man 10 years his junior in a camp boxing match to settle a difference of opinion.

About 500 prisoners with technical skills were moved from Kiangwan to camps in Japan in mid-1943. Among this group were Jasper Treadway and Roy Madden, radio officers of the *Harrison.* Treadway had known some of the Wake Island civilians in camp from a brief stint early in 1941 as a relief operator for Pan American Airways at their facility on the island. Now, he found himself going with some of those men to Japan, rather than remaining with his *Harrison* shipmates. He spent the balance of the war working in a shipyard in Osaka and, toward the end, a steel mill at Naoetsu on the northwest coast of Kyushu.

In mid-1945, with Japan reeling from constant attacks from the air, all the military prisoners in the Shanghai area were moved north to work in factories and mines in the home islands, Korea, or Manchuria. From that point on, only small groups of Marines, Wake Island civilians, or merchant officers remained together, and it is now impossible to reconstruct who was where. This became the most difficult period of captivity for the prisoners because of the added dangers of Allied attacks, their weakened physical condition aggravated by long periods of transit in crowded ships and trains, and the possibility of last-ditch fanatical resistance which might include the execution of prisoners. All accounts agree that even the liberation of prisoners was fraught with confusion, frustration, and even danger as a few prisoners were killed by air-drops of canisters of food.

This account of the men whose lives were touched by the

President Harrison would not be complete without some attention to the fate of the 4th Marine Regiment which left Shanghai in 1941 for what the troops believed to be the safety of the Philippines. Within a few days after arriving in this "American" territory these men, led by Colonel Samuel L. Howard, were committed to the battle for the Bataan Peninsula, and later to the defense of the rocky fortress that was Corregidor.

The unit had numbered 804 men upon arrival at Olongapo, but now swelled to a much larger total, augmented by men from the Marine barracks at Olongapo and Cavite. The latter group was at battalion strength, and included a number of the replacements which Admiral Hart had quietly been withholding from Shanghai during the previous months. It is difficult to know from unit records exactly how many men were now in the 4th Marines; one account says 1,440, and suggests that perhaps 50 were to die on Bataan and Corregidor. Marine Corps sources later indicated that 105 Marines were captured on Bataan and 1,283 on Corregidor for a total of 1,388 which can be equated roughly with the entire Marine presence in the Philippines.

The stories of the military campaigns for Bataan and Corregidor, the capitulation of American forces, and the infamous "Death March" have been told so often and so well that it would serve no purpose to repeat any of them here. But it may be useful to look briefly at a comparison between the captivity of the Marines in the Philippines and that of the Marines in China. The initial and obvious conclusion to be drawn from such a comparison is that the men of the 4th Marines would have fared much better had they been captured in Shanghai rather than in the Philippines.

On Luzon these Marines were confined largely at such notorious camps as O'Donnell, Bilbid, and Cabanatuan; in these overcrowded hell holes there were as many as 60,000 prisoners from all services. Later the Marines were scattered farther afield. In late 1942 a group of prisoners was transferred to Davao Penal Colony on Mindanao to work on a plantation. Even though conditions here were much better than at the camps on Luzon, 10 men led by three officers of the 4th Marines escaped in April 1943, and made their way into the back country of the large southern island. One of the group was the famous Army aviator, Ed Dyess, who stayed with the group until July when he was taken to Australia by submarine. The rest of the group fought as part of a guerilla band headed by American Army officers for the next six months before being evacuated by a submarine in November.

Other relocated Marines were not as lucky. At Puerto Princesa on the island of Palawan the prisoners were required to work on the construction of an airfield. Escape attempts were common at this prison, reflecting the brutal treatment received by the prisoners during their two-and-a-half-year stay. Finally at the end of 1944, when the Japanese sighted a large American invasion convoy offshore, the guards systematically executed prisoners. Many of the men in this camp were massacred, including 23 men of the 4th Marines.

Toward the end of the war, as the Japanese were unable to maintain overseas supply lines, most of the men of the 4th Regiment were moved northward on the "hell ships," along with other prisoners, to Japan and Manchuria. But other Marine prisoners remained in the Philippines where they were liberated by American troops early in 1945. For these men the war had ended, but for those moved north the worst of their treatment still lay ahead.

The difference in treatment of prisoners at the Shanghai camps and those in the Philippine camps can best be seen in the survival rate of the two Marine groups. For the North China Marines at Woosung and Kiangwan the survival rate was 96%, while in the various camps in the Philippines it was 65% for Marines and 58% for prisoners of all services; in each case the rate covers later experiences in Japan or other northern locations as well. Furthermore, Colonel White estimates that no more than 35 men, military and civilian, died in the two Shanghai POW camps out of a total of about 1,600 imprisoned there.

The officers of the *Harrison* were fortunate to have been imprisoned with the well-disciplined and well-staffed North China Marines. Indeed, the rescuers may well have become the rescued in this relationship. An internal comparison bears out how well the officers fared. As prisoners of war in a military camp which witnessed torture at the hands of a man later convicted as a war criminal, the officers of the *Harrison*, with a median age of 40, all survived the war. At the same time only about 91% of the unlicensed personnel of the ship, with a median age of 37, survived the war, most in the civilian detention camps in and around Shanghai, with perhaps as many as 20 crewmembers not confined at all.

Although credit should go to the North China Marines for the role they played in the prison camps, the officers of the unit were not sure they were heroes in any sense. Some thought they might ultimately be court martialled for surrendering or for not making efforts to escape. Something needs to be said at this point about the effect of an act of surrender, both on military careers and on public opinion. A brief discussion of the issues raised by the capture of the personnel of the *Wake, Peterel, Harrison*, and North China Marines will help in understanding this problem.

After escaping from Shanghai the 4th Marines spent only a brief time in the field in the Philippines before being forced to withdraw to Corregidor and captivity. (U.S. Naval Institute)

Chapter 7

Surrender and Escape: The Issues

One of the most sensitive issues that the military establishment faces is how to recognize and reward, if deemed appropriate, the service of individuals while in captivity. Nearly 45 years after the end of World War II the issues of surrender and/or survival still generate strong emotional reactions in the American political arena, periodically renewed by the experience of two more wars and by the peacetime incidents of captivity in the *Pueblo* and *Mayaguez* incidents, as well as the case of the embassy hostages in Tehran. Professional and public opinion remains ambivalent about recognition for captivity, even in the 1988 awarding of the medal for ex-prisoners of war.

A number of imprisoned officers received decorations after World War II, but generally these awards were for service in defending American positions before surrendering to an overwhelmingly superior enemy force. Among those at Woosung in this category were Major Devereux and Commander Cunningham, each of whom was awarded the Navy Cross for his role in the defense of Wake Island where 96 of the defenders died. Imprisoned elsewhere in camps in Formosa, Japan, and Manchuria, apart from his 4th Marine Regiment, was Colonel Samuel Howard who won the Navy Cross for his leadership in the defense of Bataan and Corregidor where his unit lost 4% of its men in battle and another 30% in captivity.

But for those who offered no resistance and thus lost no men in surrendering in the face of overwhelming numbers, there were no such high honors. Colonel William Ashurst was awarded the Legion of Merit for his role in helping his men survive in captivity. His citation read:

> *Enduring the most trying and humiliating conditions in his valiant efforts to mitigate the suffering and sustain the morale of his fellow prisoners, he was instrumental in lowering the mortality rate of internees. A courageous and stouthearted officer, Colonel*

Ashurst by his self-sacrificing devotion to his fellow man throughout the long period of imprisonment while suffering from poor health and hardships imposed by the enemy, upheld the highest traditions of the United States Naval Service.

While this is an accurate assessment of Ashurst's contribution, it was obviously not considered uncommonly brave behavior in Washington as it earned only the Legion of Merit which has often been called "the colonels' good conduct medal." Significantly, Dr. Foley who did not surrender any troops in North China but who was exposed to substantial physical abuse, was awarded the Navy Distinguished Service Medal, just below the Navy Cross in precedence, as well as the Bronze Star and Purple Heart.

A parallel exists with merchant marine decorations and awards. During World War II President Franklin D. Roosevelt authorized the bestowing of two significant awards, the Merchant Marine Distinguished Service Medal for individual officers and seamen and the Gallant Ship Award for individual ships. The ships and/or men who received these awards during the war-- and this comment in no way minimizes the heroic quality of their actions--were armed, they engaged in self defense, and they shot at the enemy. By way of contrast, the merchant vessels represented at Woosung and other camps in the Far East--the *President Harrison*, the *Malama*, the *Vincent*, and the *Admiral Y. S. Williams*--were ships which had left the United States in peacetime, unarmed and unescorted. Three of the ships had been scuttled or grounded to prevent their falling into Japanese hands, and the fourth was torpedoed. Yet none of these ships in the eyes of the War Shipping Administration was a "gallant ship" and no one in their crews displayed "distinguished service."

To the typical merchant seaman, this lack of recognition would have meant little. Such men, unlike military personnel, have not operated under a code of conduct that expects them to resist surrender while the means to fight are still available, or to make every effort to escape and return to duty. But to military men, the message is clear; surrender carries a stigma. That stigma was even at work in their dealings with their captors. Japanese guards told American prisoners that they held in contempt men who would surrender rather than fight on to the death; such behavior was contrary to *bushido*, the code of the warrior. This attitude of contempt made the Japanese less concerned with humanitarian treatment of prisoners than one would normally expect from a country with a long military tradition. In a curious inconsistency, however, those who surrendered without a fight, the North China Marines and the crew of the *Wake*, received essentially the same treatment in the Shanghai camps as did those who surrendered after determined resistance, the defenders of Wake Island.

In what would appear to be another curious inconsistency, the Japanese attempted to extract promises from prisoners of war that they would not attempt to escape--the concept of parole in its original sense. Traditionally, captured fighting men have been expected to make such efforts, and seemingly the Japanese would have respected this attitude. After the war, by Executive Order 10631, the *Code of Conduct* for American fighting men was promulgated as doctrine on this matter. It included these statements: "I will make every effort to escape and to aid others to escape. I will accept neither parole nor special favors from the enemy." But even before this principle was codified those who were captured were expected to try to escape and otherwise to be difficult prisoners who required the attention of large numbers of enemy soldiers as guards.

At Woosung this issue came to a head early in the imprisonment of the American and British naval and marine personnel. After the first escape attempt at that prison camp, the Japanese attempted to get all the prisoners to sign a no-escape pledge. Sir Mark Young was the only British officer in the camp at that time since Polkinghorn had been locked up for his suspected role in the escape attempt. Young, by all accounts one of the most universally admired and liked men in camp, ordered the British ratings not to sign, for which he received harsh treatment in solitary confinement. Colonel Ashurst took the opposite position; he told American servicemen that they could sign inasmuch as they would be signing under duress and their promises not to escape would have no standing in law.

Thus, although the British had far fewer men in the Shanghai prison camps than did the Americans, they seem to have outperformed their allies in displays of official insistence on proper procedures, as well as in raw courage. This disparity was evident not only in the matter of parole, but in attitudes toward surrender as well, in that the *Peterel* crewmen were all battered survivors when captured whereas the American naval personnel, outnumbered by the same ratio, all came through unscathed by not resisting.

This situation later created some ill feeling between the two navies. Polkinghorn was awarded the Distinguished Service Cross for his courage, but none of his crewmen received any citations. The British naval historian Desmond Wettern in 1960 angrily criticized his government for not adequately decorating these crewmen, arguing that the omission was a deliberate attempt to avoid embarrassing the American crew of the *Wake*.

The *Wake* episode, like the surrender of 200 Marines in North China without firing a shot, was awkward--indeed, even embarrassing--for both military commanders and historians. But the most discomforting aspect of these instances of laying down of arms was the absence of any of the support or relief that military units have a right to expect, particularly in fight-to-the-death situations. Even Custer at the Little Bighorn anticipated a relief column. No hope for any such support could have existed in China where the situation was beyond untenable; it had become unthinkable.

American fighting men, thank God, are not the fanatics about self destruction that the Japanese showed themselves to be in World War II. Life is still sacred in our military tradition, and, while the unofficial expectation (later made official in the *Code of Conduct*) is that a fighting man is prepared to give his life for his country, that ultimate gift should be made only when some clear purpose can be achieved or when some hope of improving a situation exists. All the military captives of Shanghai had been put into the hazardous position in which they found themselves on December 8th through the reckless gambling of planners at distant locations. Under those circumstances, saving life seems to make sense.

Of course, these same circumstances prevailed for Polkinghorn and the *Peterel*. Why, then, did the captain of that ship do what he did? Perhaps he was simply being pragmatic, assuming that he could get better treatment for his men from the Japanese if they resisted with a show of force. Or perhaps it was more a matter of principle; he may have been making a personal statement that remembered Dunkerque and anticipated Hong Kong and Singapore, a statement about true British resolve and courage.

Smith, on the other hand, had no options to exercise. The swiftness with which his ship was overrun left no time for notification of, much less deliberation over, the demand for surrender. To his credit, Smith redeemed himself--if, indeed, he needed to--by his miraculous escape to Chungking.

If there is any disappointment to be expressed over American prisoner behavior at Shanghai, it may be in the lack of escape activity on the part of the Marines. Perhaps their six-month-long ploy to go home as diplomatic personnel may have weakened their self-image as fighting men. In any case, only one Marine managed to break out of prison and get away: Corporal Jerold Story who was part of the escape engineered by the disabled 51-year-old Columbus D. Smith. Several others participated in the two unsuccessful attempts by the 45-year-old Commander Cunningham. But no Marine officers or even sergeants made any escape attempts at Woosung or Kiangwan, and it was not until they were shipped north by train in 1945 that any of these younger leaders slipped away.

Although this discussion has raised the question of what kind of behavior a nation can realistically expect from its military personnel who are captured while in combat, it should not be necessary to point out the potential unfairness and inappropriateness of criticisms of prisoner behavior made by those who have not gone through the experience of confinement themselves. Perhaps it is fairer for those of us who are among the uninitiated to ask, what might have been done to encourage or assist more men to escape?

Inasmuch as the only successful escape from the military prisons in Shanghai was accomplished by Smith, an old China hand who knew the language but nevertheless was forced to improvise completely on his trek to Chungking for lack of specific contacts, it is necessary to ask, what kind of intelligence or underground organization existed in China? Some sort of Chinese-run organization existed in Shanghai in which the *Peterel's* elusive radioman participated, but it is not clear just what this group accomplished. The Navy had its own counter-intelligence organization, the U.S. Naval Group, China, headed by Rear Admiral Milton E. "Mary" Miles. This group claimed to have 2,500 American operatives in China, mostly Marines or Navy men, plus 80,000 native guerillas. It took credit for coastwatching and other activities on the coast of China which was largely in Japanese hands. It even claimed that it ran a 100-bed Navy hospital from which the lights of Shanghai could be seen. If this is the case, it is difficult to understand why prisoners at Woosung and Kiangwan, who received Shanghai newspapers and food parcels with some regularity, could not have been contacted and escape assistance provided by these agents and facilities. Thus, the whole question of the rather passive behavior of Marines in the Shanghai camps becomes even more puzzling.

In any case, the Japanese benefitted from having manageable prisoners. They had anticipated that their enemies would fight rather than surrender. When instead they found themselves with a number of captives, they reacted with frustration and inconsistency, scorning and abusing those Allied fighting men who surrendered but nevertheless expecting them to be docile prisoners who would take themselves completely out of the war. When the few escape attempts were made, the Japanese were provoked into such irrational actions as treating the Woosung escapees as deserters from the Japanese Army, depriving them of their right to be treated as military captives, and jailing them at Ward Road as common criminals under long sentences. However, in other places in the Far East such escapes might have led to executions of those involved; once again the civilizing influence of Shanghai on the Japanese was evident.

With civilian prisoners the Japanese had no such misreading of motives as they did with military men who had surrendered. For this and other reasons, life was not as difficult for civilian internees as it was for military captives. Particularly was this true in the Shanghai area where the local residents were fully acclimated to the political as well as the physical climate from living with a Japanese military presence over a four-year period. As David Bergamini, writing in *Japan's Imperial Conspiracy* said of these internees, "They coped with the same captors, the same latent brutality and smouldering hate, but they were not despised by the Japanese for being soldiers who had surrendered."

How the unlicensed crewmembers from the *President Harrison* would fit into these special circumstances of wartime Shanghai we shall see next.

Chapter 8

The Crew as Internees

Returning to Shanghai as captives in late January 1942, was not as traumatic for the crew of the *President Harrison* as it would have been immediately following the grounding at Shawei-shan. The intervening six weeks had given the members of the crew an opportunity to adjust to their new role as prisoners. It had also given them an awareness of how badly the war was going for the United States and its allies in the Far East, and of how much worse things might have been for all of them.

The internment of the crew in Shanghai took place through an evolutionary process, rather than by a single, dramatic action, with the process even changing directions at times. When the ship first arrived at the Jardine Matheson wharf the crew was subject to considerable restraint in the form of being kept aboard to continue working with the salvage crew. Later, much more freedom would be granted to the crewmembers, and still later that freedom would give way to genuine incarceration.

When the ship first arrived at the dock, in order to alert whatever remained of the American President Lines staff in Shanghai to her presence and status, the passenger agent on board, Ed Wise, surreptitiously passed notes ashore to onlookers, asking them to contact the company. In time these messages did reach Henry F. Kay, the APL general agent, but it was likely that the presence of the ship back in Shanghai was already well known to the American and European community. Kay had earlier learned of the ship's fate at Shaweishan through the Chinese captain of a tender that had once been owned by APL.

The *President Harrison* remained at the wharf with crew aboard for about six weeks while the Japanese, in addition to their repair work, decided what to do with the vessel and her heterogenous personnel. Henry Behrens, a 22-year-old ordinary seaman, recalls that period.

> *During the month and a half we were prisoners on*
> *the docked **Harrison** we had many visitors. Most of*

them were high naval officials who came and looked over the ship. Sometimes the crewmembers were reviewed by the officials. At one instance when we were lined up I stood at the front of the line. The admiral singled me out, walked up with his interpreter, and began asking me questions. He asked me my name, about my family (they always asked questions concerning the family), my native state, and my age. After I told him my age, he mumbled to the interpreter who passed the message to me, "Poor boy, it will be a long time before he sees home."

A senior clerk in the purser's department, Jack Hallinan, remembers that for a while the Japanese made plans to have a skeleton crew of about 35 men from the crew sail the ship to Japan. He was concerned because he was listed as purser on the prospective crew list which had been drawn up. For some reason, however, this plan was not carried out, and when the crewmembers left the ship in Shanghai in two groups on March 5 and March 12, 1942, they were not to go aboard her again.

Up until this point no distinction had yet been made between officers and crew of the *Harrison* in terms of any punishment to be meted out for the trouble the ship's grounding had caused her captors. The Japanese were in no hurry to acquire additional captives; they knew that captivity had its costs for the captor in money and manpower. Japan clearly could not have imprisoned all her potential enemies in the Shanghai area. The International Settlement and the French Settlement of the city, long encircled by the Japanese, now had been occupied by Imperial troops. But it was physically impossible to lock up all the enemy nationals in those sections of the city--all the British, American, Dutch, Belgians, and other nationalities representing the Allied forces engaged in war against the Rome-Berlin-Tokyo Axis powers. One hundred thousand recent European Jewish refugees and an equal number of stateless White Russians from World War I swelled the population of the city to about 3.5 million people, most of whom, including the native Chinese, did not like the Japanese. Thus the only practical course of action for the Japanese in Shanghai in 1942 was to imprison Allied military personnel, keep track of diplomatic and other official personnel, and let everyone else remain free.

On this basis, the captain and officers of the *Harrison* were eventually singled out as military personnel. Although it appears that only a few of the officers actually were Naval Reservists, the ship herself had long been designated as a Naval Reserve vessel. Furthermore, her recent use as a military transport under the operational control of the Navy gave the Japanese further justification to regard the officers as military personnel. As a result, it was no surprise when these 19 men were sent from the ship to the Kiangwan naval base in mid-March, later to join the Marines at Woosung as military captives.

Why the crew of the *Harrison* was excused from this confinement remains a mystery. In parallel cases, the crew of the *Malama*, another scuttled American ship, was imprisoned along with her officers at Woosung, and most of the crew of the *Admiral Y. S. Williams*, the other scuttled merchant ship, had been imprisoned at Kowloon, although, inexplicably, some men in this crew were later repatriated. Furthermore, even civilian construction workers from Wake Island had been confined at Woosung. While admittedly these workers had participated in the defense of the island, so had the crew of the *Harrison* participated in the hostile act of destruction that had angered the Japanese. One can only speculate that, if there indeed was a reason for the inconsistency on the part of the Japanese in defining military captives, it may have reflected the large number of clearly non-combatant people aboard in the steward's department, or it may have grown out of the ethnic diversity within the crew of the ship.

This diversity continued to puzzle the Japanese. While they were accustomed to the multi-national population of Shanghai, their perception of Americans reflected only their contact with the predominantly white Anglo-Saxon military, diplomatic and commercial types who ventured to the Orient to represent the interests of the United States, along with the missionaries spreading Christianity. Perhaps the 40 or so Asian, Black, and Latino crewmembers, plus the 10 men born in countries now part of greater Germany, caused the Japanese to decide that granting freedom for all was simpler than trying to sort though the philosophic justification for releasing some while detaining others. In any case, after leaving the ship the unlicensed crew of the *Harrison* joined the civilian population of Shanghai in remaining free to move about the city.

The American population of the city was probably about 1,000 at this point, compared to about 6,500 British and 500 Dutch. At the request of the State Department most business-men had sent their families home or to the Philippines or Australia, but there were still a number of women and children left in Shanghai. Later, when internment came, some would go to camps with their menfolk; in other cases families would be split with mothers and small children remaining at large while fathers and older children went into camps. Although the large American companies that had been prominent in the commercial life of the city--Standard Oil, National City Bank, IT & T, and the like--had been forced to cease operating, there was still much to be done by their employees in shutting down and in keeping track of holdings until such time as they would be back in operation, an optimistic dream that began to look less likely as the early months of the war passed with no good news for the Allies.

Under the freedom granted by the Japanese the crewmem-bers of the *Harrison* were treated essentially as wards of the Swiss consul, Emile Fontanel, a man who was to play a stabil-izing role in the protection of foreigners during the war -- although some internees felt that the consulate benefitted finan-cially and unnecessarily from this role. The consulate in the French Settlement became the center of sustenance for the crew of the *Harrison*.

It has always been difficult to determine exactly who was on board the *President Harrison* at Shaweishan and, consequently, which crewmembers were in Shanghai at liberty and, later, in confinement. The original crew list showed 164 names. But records available from the Shanghai internment and from post-war court cases suggest strongly that three of the people on that list were not on board at Shaweishan, and that four additional people not on the crew list had joined the ship along the way, making a total of 165 crewmembers on board. Three were killed in the grounding. The records of the APL general agent in Shanghai showed 142 crewmembers interned later in the city and 20 officers imprisoned at Woosung/Kiangwan. (Today, 143 crewmembers and 19 officers appears to be the correct count; in both cases the numbers deal only with survivors, and disregard those who had died.) So it seems reasonably certain that 165 crewmembers had been on board the ship, plus the captain and the passenger agent.

The post-war court cases, in which thousands of dollars in back bonus payments for each crewmember were at stake, became in time the best way to determine specifically the names of those who were captives in Shanghai. Even so, three members of the engine department, two of whom were known to be in a particular camp in Shanghai, apparently never applied for the bonus. Whether they returned to the States with the rest of the crew after the war can therefore not be determined.

While no mass internments took place in Shanghai throughout most of 1942, life in this once glamorous city was no longer as comfortable for Europeans and Americans. Shortages of food and housing resulted from the Japanese occupation, and restrictions on free movement within and in-and-out of the city were imposed. And yet, life went on much as before for the people of the city. The affluent tried to live as well as possible, and the poor tried only to live. The newspapers reported more than 500 beggars died in the streets one November night; a monthly total was over 4,700.

The once-dazzling nightlife of Shanghai continued but at a reduced level, enjoyed primarily by the Germans, Italians, French, and stateless White Russians, and monitored by the Japanese. However, the romantic nightclub operator, Joe Farrens--a Far Eastern counterpart to the storied "Rick" of "Casablanca"--ran afoul of the authorities, and was imprisoned and later died in the infamous Bridge House, the former apartment building on Szechuan Road which housed the headquarters of the *Kempeitai* or secret police.

Confinement in Bridge House was the most dreaded fate awaiting Allied nationals in Shanghai. While none of the *Harrison* crew experienced this fate, the early military escapees from Woosung spent time here before going to Ward Road jail. One of these escapees, Commander Cunningham from Wake Island, later reported that there was an American President Lines employee named W. G. MacDonald detained at Bridge House, a man he assumed was suspected of having ties to Naval Intelligence. The most famous American to survive Bridge House was J. B. Powell, editor of the *China Weekly Review*, who was repatriated in 1943 in such poor condition that he had to have parts of both legs amputated. This nefarious installation was certainly a place to be avoided at all costs.

For the crew of the *Harrison* the challenge now was to each individual's resourcefulness in finding a place to stay, something to do to stay busy and out of trouble, and discovering a way to beat the system. Fortunately, merchant seamen, far more than military personnel, have learned to survive on their own resources. This background helped the crew adjust to this strange new lifestyle.

A number of the crew stayed at the Foreign YMCA on Bubbling Well Road, across from the racetrack where the horses continued to run. Some doubled up with others from the ship to take apartments in the city. A few crewmembers were married to local women during this time, while others found live-in female companions--what the 4th Marines used to call "shackmates."

Work was available for those who wanted it, but there seemed to be little incentive to earn additional money. A few of the waiters from the ship may have gone to work in restaurants or night clubs. A room steward began trading in bicycle tires and aspirin, both scarce commodities, but he was soon put out of business by the Japanese who frowned on black market activities. For the most part, crewmembers spent their time in purely recreational activities, ranging from shooting pool at the Y to attending the opera. A few seamen with prescience may have cultivated important local people who did not appear to be likely candidates for any upcoming general internment. While it lasted, it was a remarkably pleasant interlude.

As a part of the effort to keep track of enemy nationals the Japanese after a few months issued armbands which the *Harrison* crewmembers were required to wear. Made of heavy red material, reportedly from draperies of the Italian Club, these armbands were imprinted in black with a large A for American, under which an inch-high individual serial number appeared for each person. Along with the issuing of armbands went the imposition of an eight p.m. curfew.

During this initial confusing period with so many enemy nationals at large it would not have been difficult to slip away from Shanghai and make good an escape. A few Americans did so; no one from the *Harrison* tried, but such diverse types as a banker from National City Bank and the two firemen from the crew of the *Wake* managed to make it out of China. Generally to succeed in such an effort required money, friends and a knowledge of the language. It was unlikely that any *Harrison* crewmember had enough of those escape ingredients to consider making the attempt. Besides, life in Shanghai was not all that bad, at least compared to life at Shaweishan.

The prospect of repatriation was a constant dream for tens of thousands of people in Shanghai early in the war, including the crew of the *Harrison*. But such repatriations on exchange ships were infrequent, and only a small portion of those who wanted to go home could actually do so. One sailing occurred in the summer of 1942 while the crew of the *Harrison* was still at liberty. The Italian liner *Conte Verde* went from Shanghai to Lorenco Marques in Portugese Mozambique where she exchanged her American repatriates for Japanese civilians, largely diplomats, who had been brought from New York on the chartered Swedish liner *Gripsholm*. The *Asama Maru* brought other diplomats to this African port from Yokohama, Hong Kong, and Saigon. In addition to her passengers the *Gripsholm* also brought out relief packages for the military POWs; in time, the name of this ship became synonomous with humanity and decency in a Pacific war in which captives had experienced very little of those qualities.

Jack Hallinan and Henry F. Kay each recall that the *Harrison* crew was once given serious consideration for repatriation on a proposed September 1942 trip, to the point of being issued a special cash draw to enable the seamen to buy whatever gear they would need for the long trip home. But the voyage failed to materialize for them, perhaps because there were other Americans in Shanghai who had "earned" the right to go home ahead of the crew by virtue of having done whatever the State Department had asked of them, particularly in sending their families home before the war.

As noted earlier, however, some inexplicable repatriations did take place. The four Marines from the administrative detail of the 4th Regiment were allowed to leave from Woosung, and the executive officer of the *Wake* and the retired Marine major from Peking were also sent home. Otherwise, the bulk of the people on the first voyage home were diplomats and State Department personnel.

Working out of the Swiss consulate, APL agent Henry F. Kay served as liaison and paymaster for the crew of the *Harrison*. Ship's clerk Hallinan, who sometimes assisted in this work, recalled that there was virtually an APL branch within the consulate. However, he did not want to be too closely identified with these activities since, as the crew was learning, maintaining a low profile was a valuable guideline for anyone under the purview of the Japanese.

The ship's officers at Woosung/Kiangwan were apparently not paid through the Swiss consulate, but the unlicensed crewmembers were paid regularly while they were free in Shanghai and even later for special needs when they were interned in camps. The payments were authorized by Kay and made by the Swiss consulate; individual crewmembers signed for their cash draw and Kay countersigned for the company. During the first few months the money was provided by a subscription of the Relief Finance Committee of the American Association of Shanghai; payment was $1,000 a month in Chinese National dollars. The rate for these dollars, commonly known as "Mex," had been three to one before the war, and was probably in the 20 to 30 to one range at this point. Later, after the State Department was able to make arrangements with the Swiss government to subsidize the payments, the equivalent of $65 a month American was provided to each crewmember. By way of comparison, most of the low-paying jobs on the ship carried a wage of $77.50 a month at that time, without overtime, bonuses, or tips.

Inflation was a serious problem in China during the war, but by having their payments pegged to American dollars the crewmembers were generally better off than other civilian detainees who had no such subsidy. The Chinese National dollars were soon replaced by CRB (Central Reserve Bank) currency of the puppet government installed by the Japanese, and this money declined rapidly in value as the war went on. At the time of internment in camps in January 1943, the crew was given CRB yuan worth 42.5 to one in American dollars. At the end of the war, according to Henry F. Kay, the ratio was 200,000 to one for this Japanese money and 200 to one for the old Chinese nationalist money. Other sources cite other ratios which vary considerably. George Laycock's houseboy reported that 12,000 to one was the rate for CRB in late spring of 1945, but a menu preserved by Howard Allred, showing prices in both American dollars and CRB on September 21, 1945, shows the rate as 138,462 to one.

Meticulous records were kept of the amounts paid to each crewmember. The largest total amount received by any crewmember was 19,536,736 CRB which went to oiler William Smith while in camp, equivalent to $97.68 American by the post-war exchange rate reported by Kay. Of course, many of the payments were made at lower exchange rates, so it is impossible to know what the real total of this particular financial support amounted to in American money. An average rate of perhaps 10,000 to one might produce a fairly realistic assessment of the cost to the State Department and APL of the payments to Smith: $1,953.67 American.

The strange odyssey of the *Harrison* crewmembers on the streets of Shanghai lasted thoughout 1942. During this time the Japanese-controlled English language daily newspapers of the city kept the crew informed of the progress of the war. At this point very little manipulation of the news was necessary. Accurate accounts of Japanese victories spoke for themselves. Sometimes stories with surprising detail and objectivity were reported, including the matter-of-fact notation that Captain Pierson of the *Harrison* had been transferred to Zentsuji prison in Japan. The death notices for two crewmembers also appeared in the newspapers. It must have been an incongruous feeling for these American seamen to be at large in an enemy-controlled foreign city, watching the war from afar, and having no idea of what the months and years ahead might bring. Life, however, would soon change, and this pseudo-freedom would give way to real captivity.

The beginning of 1943 marked a turn in the war, in that the southerly drive of the Japanese had been halted with the retaking of Papua and Guadacanal by the Allies. It also marked a change in attitude by Japanese officials toward the laissez-faire detainment of enemy nationals in Shanghai.

The first internment of civilians had occurred in November 1942, when a group of several hundred men, prominent in business affairs in Shanghai, was put into a camp on Haiphong Road that had once been part of the U.S. Marine Corps headquarters. These men were initially thought to be political prisoners or hostages taken by the Japanese to insure proper behavior by the rest of the Allied nationals in Shanghai, but as later internments occurred this interpretation no longer appeared accurate. All told, 35 different "assemblies" of internees were convened over the course of more than a year to gather up all the civilians whom the Japanese wanted interned.

At the end of January 1943, most such westerners, including the crew of the *Harrison*, were ordered into "civil assembly areas" which were detention camps. The members of the crew received individual notification by mail to report to the Bund for transportation to Pootung, across the river, where the old British-American Tobacco Company warehouse had been designated as such a center. Each individual was permitted to bring a limited amount of personal belongings.

Consistent with their view that Orientals were all brothers in the struggle against the West, the Japanese did not require any members of the *Harrison* crew who were of Chinese, Korean, or Japanese ancestry to be confined during the internment. As a result, at least 12 crewmen remained at large during the balance of the war, although several others of Oriental extraction did choose to enter a camp. Apparently a few other crewmembers for health or other reasons also remained at large, at least part of the time. The location of each *Harrison* crewmember in Shanghai was provided in a letter written by Henry F. Kay to the Swiss consul in March of 1943. This letter was introduced into the post-war court cases, but it is evidently no longer extant. Consequently, it is impossible to know where every one of the crewmembers was located during the balance of the time spent in Shanghai, although reconstructed lists do account for most of the crew.

All accounts of Pootung indicate that it was a well-run camp, at least early in its history before food supplies became critical. The Japanese commandant was K. Tsuchiya, formerly the consul in Seattle who had been exchanged on the *Gripsholm* late in 1942. Consular guards, rather than military personnel, were utilized, and for the most part they left the internees to manage their own affairs. Initially, five Americans and 10 Britishers were designated as leaders of sections of 20 men each, but later the number of internees reached 1,100, with 200 Americans, 800 British, and about 100 Dutch.

Physically the buildings could be described as substantial, but rundown. A three-story section stood in the center, flanked by two-story wings on each side. The buildings were constructed of brick, but the interiors were of wooden frame construction, infested with vermin. A high concrete wall topped with barbed wire surrounded the buildings. With 1,100 residents the premises were quite crowded; later the Japanese allowed the prisoners to convert an adjacent field into a baseball diamond and recreation area, which relieved some of the pressure on living space.

Food was adequate at the outset, but later declined significantly in quantity and quality. As Jack Hallinan recalled,

> We lived on rice, buffalo stew, ribbon fish, beet root, a kind of spinach, American Red Cross cracked wheat, corn maize, bread, tea. All water was boiled. For a period we could get small amounts of peanut butter, eggs, small cakes which would be charged back through the American government. I received a total of five parcels of 12.5 pounds each of canned necessities from the American Red Cross. A robust eater would be hungry.

Other crewmembers have pointed out that the cracked wheat was from four-year-old relief supplies, infested with weevils. One observer recalled that the water buffalo were dragged into camp whole, and the carcasses were then butchered. Fortunately for all the internees, the *Harrison*'s steward's department contained specialists in all aspects of food preparation. E. L. Roberts, the second steward, and John Burney, the second butcher, were instrumental in organizing and operating the food service at the camp.

Most of the crewmembers in later years were realistic, even philosophical, about the food at Pootung. Fireman Mike Barassa told an interviewer, "The food was horrible, but we couldn't really expect them to run out and find us pot roast or something like that." Another fireman, Gil Monreal, recalls, "The food was prepared by our cooks and was meager but enough to keep body and soul together. As the war progressed Japan's setbacks were reflected in our food supply." Able seaman Howard Allred, who was later in two other camps, remembers, "One lingering effect of the prolonged insufficient nutrition was eventual disinterest in food. The first six months in Pootung was the toughest before the stomach shrank to accommodate the limited food..."

Sanitary facilities, while not primitive, were quite limited at

Pootung. Only a few water taps, toilets, and showers existed for the 1,100 men. Initially hot water was available, but later as fuel became scarce this luxury disappeared. Several doctors were among the internees, but their effectiveness in treating common ailments such as malaria or dysentery was restricted by a lack of medication. Seriously ill patients were transferred to Shanghai hospitals for treatment; several *Harrison* seamen were so treated, including oiler Ervin O'Neale who had chronic back and neck problems while in camp.

In the important area of recreation and morale old-fashioned ingenuity made the camp a more tolerable environment for everyone. Sports were an important outlet. The baseball field provided for more than one sport; it was used for soccer and cricket as well. The ship's barber, William Levy, found a railroad axle with wheels that could be used for weightlifting. Other recreational activities included a band whose music became very popular, classes and lectures on a wide variety of subjects, a dramatics group, and a somewhat limited library.

Contact with the outside world came through infrequent mail and relief packages, along with the Shanghai papers which were available in camp. For a while a clandestine radio receiver was in operation from which news reports were distributed, but on a tip the Japanese eventually located the set and sent several people who had smuggled parts of it into camp off to Bridge House, the notorious Japanese police facility in Shanghai. This action was particularly disturbing because it indicated that there were people in camp who were cooperating with the Japanese to receive favors or special treatment.

One of the most complete accounts of life in the Pootung camp was that written many years later by George Laycock, a young American affiliated with St. John's University and the Episcopal Church in China. As one of the original section leaders and later as the elected American representative to the camp commandant, Laycock was in a good position to view all aspects of life in camp. His unpublished manuscript entitled "Prisoner in Cathay" which described his experiences contains much useful information.

He had, however, one blind spot--an ongoing dislike and distrust for the crew of the *Harrison* whom he called "a tough bunch of men if ever there was one." His dislike can be explained only inferentially through such statements as this:

The unlicensed crewmembers of the *Harrison* were at liberty for almost a year in Shanghai, even in wartime a cosmopolitan and sophisticated city. (Naval Historical Center)

The Lunghwa internment center was a functional site with little adornment. (Howard Allred)

The Chapei camp was a former college campus. Pictures of the camps deteriorated in captivity, as did the prisoners. (Howard Allred)

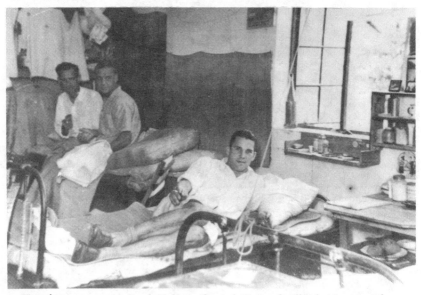

Harrison crewmen Fred Kulper (l) and Howard Allred (r) entertain a Russian friend in their room at Chapei. (Howard Allred)

"Several were professed Communists and did everything they could to stir up trouble. It was with these Americans (although many had been foreign born) that I had the most trouble." Captain Pierson and APL officials would probably have been amused at this opinion. Laycock may simply have lived a sheltered life in which he had never been exposed to the partisan opinions of West Coast union seamen, opinions that did not seem so disturbing to those accustomed to hearing them.

Explaining that he had run for the post of American representative at the urging of others to defeat "a Communist American seaman" who was running for the office, Laycock nevertheless eventually made use of *Harrison* personnel in his "administration." Jack Hallinan, the senior ship's clerk, served as his secretary, and Richard Burnside, a large Black who was a pantryman on the ship, functioned as an advisor/enforcer for Laycock.

Unlike the *Harrison* officers at Woosung/Kiangwan who were quite inconspicuous to fellow prisoners who later wrote accounts of captivity, the unlicensed crewmen of the ship were noticed, with reactions varying from awe to humor by those who wrote about their experiences in the internment camps. George Laycock's observations have already been noted. John S. Potter, an American real estate executive who shared room 13 at Pootung with 75 other men, recalled such things as the colorful tattoo on the chest of able seamen Blackie Kelleher, the resourceful meals provided by second steward Ernest Roberts, the imaginative baking of chief pantryman Daniel Holden, and the aversion to work of a ship's baker who shall remain nameless. Arch Carey, a British employee of the Shell Oil Company, recalled that at the Lincoln Avenue camp, a facility for those who were elderly and/or ill, the "best handyman in the camp" and an expert knife sharpener was an "amiable old man" whom he identified as a carpenter from the *President Harrison*, a man who later died. This man was clearly not the ship's carpenter, Anders Mortensen, a younger man confined at Lungwha; it is difficult to determine whom he might have been. Henry Stolz, a nightwatchman in his mid-50s, was the only crewman known to have been at Lincoln Avenue, but he survived the war. In any case, this unnamed old man was remembered by Carey as a "good Samaritan."

A group tribute to the competence of the men of the

111

Harrison came at a post-war reunion of Pootung internees held in Shanghai, when they were remembered, along with internees from the local utility companies and a shipyard, as "our wonderful technicians" who "built out of scrap or junk, installations, boilers, toilets, showers, which were masterpieces." From this praise one might infer that these Shanghai residents, accustomed to having their household projects accomplished by servants and tradesmen, were out of touch with a real world that occasionally required getting one's hands dirty around the house. Perhaps even before internment began these people were "captives of Shanghai" in that their affluent expatriate living had led to an addictive dependency on others and on the system itself. Early in the internment it became clear that the *Harrison* people could be helpful to these Shanghailanders in reducing the impact of this dependency.

The *Harrison* crew was also remembered for more than its technical competence. The novelist J. G. Ballard recalls fondly the men of the *Harrison* from whom he was able to cadge belt buckles and other geegaws at Lungwha. He is quick to point out that no one in that group was the model for "Basie," the less-than-charming wheeler-dealer in *Empire of the Sun*. Such operators did exist, however. At Pootung a pair of men named Ezra and Rock carried out this role, while at the Woosung POW camp it was Sam Katz. Apparently none of these men was a seaman.

The summer of 1943 was particularly eventful for the thousands of internees in Shanghai. In late July the residents of the Pootung camp were surprised to see the Italian liner *Conte Verde*, which had been riding to a buoy in the Whangpoo since completing her exchange with the *Gripsholm* during the winter, suddenly heel over on her side and sink. Unbeknownst to the internees, Italy had just capitulated to the Allies, and the crew, rather than surrender the ship to the Japanese, had chosen to scuttle her in an act of defiance. The *Conte Verde* crew members were then arrested, and along with the Italian Marines from Shanghai were sent to the Woosung prison camp where they joned the American Marines from North China and Wake Island, and the officers from the *Harrison*.

Also unbeknownst to the internees, an exchange trip had been planned by the Japanese for later in the summer. Now the officials were forced quickly to find another ship to make the trip. In August about 1,500 lucky people found their names on the list prepared by the Swiss consul. Among this group were two people from the *Harrison*: Clara Main, the stewardess, and Ed Wise, the passenger agent who had boarded at Manila. They learned that the Japanese liner *Teia Maru* had been pressed into service as the exchange ship to gather eligible passengers from Shanghai; this vessel was the former *Aramis*, a motorship of the French Mail Line, Messageries Maritimes, which had provided service between the Mediterranean and the Far East. The other ship used in this repatriation was the *Kamakura Maru* which collected passengers at other locations in the Orient. The grossly-overloaded *Teia Maru* had 500 male passengers berthed in a cargo hold. The trip to the Portugese colony of Goa on the mainland of India to meet the *Gripsholm* turned into an extension of internment camp life with its survival-driven thievery, compounded by the presence on board of much liquor and a mysterious group of ruffian repatriates who caused a lot of trouble.

These men may have been part of the crew of the American freighter *Admiral Y. S. Williams* who were inexplicably being sent home, or even crewmen from the APL ship *President Grant*, one fifth of whose crew had been left behind in Manila when that ship had sailed abruptly the day the war began. This latter group had been at Pootung, along with the *Harrison* crew, and now these men were going home, another of the inconsistencies shown by the Japanese in handling captured merchant crews.

With the departure of these exchange ships in mid-1943 came a massive reshuffling of internees from camp to camp which affected more people than did the actual repatriation. A number of families were brought into the Shanghai area from upriver, and Pootung for the first time had women in camp. The influx of internees was absorbed by other camps which had been established around the perimeter of Shanghai, principally at Lungwha, a former college located on the south side of the city, and at Chapei, also once a college, across Soochow Creek on the north side. Additional camps included two on Great Western Road, one of which was the American country club and the other was on the site of a former ash dump for which it was named, another in a former public school on Yu Yuen Road, and those previously mentioned on Haiphong Road and Lincoln Avenue.

Personnel from the *Harrison* were assigned to most of these camps, apparently as a cadre of workers and technicians who could assist other internees in coping with their new environment. Some choice of camp was given to those crewmembers who were relocated. Approximately 20 men went from Pootung to Lungwha, about a quarter of whom later went to Chapei where they were joined by several others. Five went to Great Western Road, and one to Yu Yuen Road. This lone individual in the latter camp was Norman Jones, a waiter originally from England; perhaps his separation from his shipmates on the *Harrison* was offset by being with other Englishmen.

The new camps had unique personalities. Lungwha and Yu Yuen were primarily British, and Chapei was distinctly American. Pootung remained perhaps the most cosmopolitan, heavily British but with strong American and Dutch representation. With women sharing life in this camp with men who had already been imprisoned for months it was inevitable that pregnancies would soon be a new problem. When these occurred outside of marriage, George Laycock invariably blamed them on the men from the *Harrison*. But this stern American camp official managed to find a bit of humor in Commandant Tsuchiya's warning to him, "Meester Raycock, the Japanese Consurate General is very much worried about the irregitimate children in the camp."

Life at Lungwha has been described colorfully in J. G. Ballard's autobiographical novel, *Empire of the Sun*, and the 1988 motion picture of the same name. The camp was adjacent to an airfield, now the Shanghai International Airport, and included a stadium, reportedly built at the behest of Madame Chiang Kai Shek to induce the Olympic Committee to hold the 1940 games in Shanghai. The film contains much that is authentic, but the Lungwha scenes were filmed in Spain.

About 1,700 people were confined at Lungwha, with the *Harrison* crewmembers virtually the only Americans. Gil Monreal, the fireman, was given the responsibility for firing the boilers for hot water; he also worked in the kitchen where he found the presence of women a morale booster. He remembers,

> *The food was a little better than Pootung, but fell off sharply as the war progressed. Our diet was about the same with a form of rice gruel, called congee, for*

114

breakfast. Lunch and dinner was always the same with a stew of vegetables and, when available, very little meat. Food parcels were allowed to come in once a month. Most of the internees had connections in Shanghai and took advantage of this. Some of us with no connections had to rely on the regular rations.

Another fireman, who also assisted in the kitchen, was Mike Barassa. His memories of Lungwha were not bitter ones. He was young enough to view much of the experience as a lark. For example, he described how "we would do things to keep our sanity, you know, like sneak out to a little farm outside the camp and trade clothing for cigarettes and stuff. ... The prison camp was not all that bad." Lungwha was definitely not an escape-proof camp; five British men in one escape group were known to have reached Free China.

Able seaman Howard Allred had been briefly at Lungwha before being relocated to Chapei. He saw real differences between the camps:

Chapei was essentially an American camp. That was where the American Red Cross relief supplies went. I was amazed at the supplemental fare at Chapei vs. Pootung or Lungwha. Chapei was where the relief went as did the American tai pans of Shanghai.

Allred perceived Chapei as the camp for the American "power structure" of Shanghai. Support for this position can be seen in the fact that such people as Jimmy James, the well-known restaurateur and his family were confined here, as was Carl Mydans, the *Time-Life* journalist who edited the camp newspaper, the *Assembly Times*. Several people from the American President Lines shore staff was confined here, including Henry F. Kay, head of the Shanghai office, Ed Wise, the passenger agent who was repatriated on the second *Gripsholm* voyage, and John Carey, an assistant to Kay. In an interesting sidelight, Carey was married in Chapei to a Dutch woman at a camp wedding attended by *Harrison* crewmembers; subsequently, the Careys' first child was delivered by the ship's doctor, Claude Ray, who was also at Chapei.

Physically, Chapei may also have been the most attractive of the larger camps. It had a columned Old Main building and a quadrangle, reminiscent of American college campuses. With the presence of a number of missionaries it soon developed an extensive system of schools at all levels. The camp housed a number of families as well as single men and single women.

No civilian internees were moved from Shanghai to the mines and mills of Japan, Manchuria, and Korea. However, the men of the Haiphong Road camp were sent by train as far as Fengtai, near Peking, in late spring of 1945, where they spent the balance of the war. An interesting sidelight to this trip was the fact that it was made without attack by American aircraft which had regularly been bombing this rail line. The peaceful passage of the train was apparently arranged through the underground in Shanghai in which Jim Cuming, the at-large radioman from the *Peterel*, was an important figure. This underground was also credited with a role in the earlier escape of Smith, Woolley, and Story from Ward Road jail.

Other shifts of internees also occurred during the spring of 1945 around Shanghai. The camps on Great Western Road and Yu Yuen Road were closed, and the internees at these locations were placed in a nondescript facility in the easternmost part of the Hongkew district with the quaint name of Yangtze-Poo.

Roughly the same conclusions can be drawn about the life of the crew in the Shanghai camps as can be drawn about the officers at Woosung/Kiangwan: that they quietly put in their time, surviving--at least most of the crew did--through their resourcefulness and inner strength. Howard Allred, who has given considerable thought to his three and a half years in Shanghai, believes that the merchant seamen of that era were uniquely prepared for the hardships of crowded confinement through being basically loners--men who were accustomed to enduring long boring passages at sea, living in crowded spaces with a minimum of privacy, keeping themselves and their surroundings clean, and entertaining themselves with simple pleasures such as reading or a game of chess.

Nevertheless, while their confinement was as civilian internees and was relatively bearable compared to that of American fighting men captured in the Far East, the seamen of the *Harrison* still were exposed to deprivation and adversity far beyond anything for which their training and experience as mariners had prepared them. In spite of their ability to deal

The first repatriation from Shanghai was on the Italian liner *Conte Verde*, later scuttled in the Whangpoo River by her crew. (Howard Allred)

The exchange ship *Gripsholm* was a two-way link between the prisoners in China and the real world of the United States. (U.S. Naval Institute)

This bill for 10,000 CRB dollars might have bought a shoeshine for
Harrison crewmen at the end of the war. (Howard Allred)

The American goodwill mission made its first inspection
eal camp conditions yesterday. (Top) Major Schoyer, (foreground)
nd Lieut.-Comm. Shoemaker (centre) salute the US colours
incoln Avenue Camp. (Bottom) Left to right: Lieut. Estes, M.
Andrews (camp chairman), Capt. Levin, Lieut. Comm.
lajor Schoyer, Lieut. Cox, Lieut. "Pete" Kim, are at the
hapei Camp platform during an address to the inte

This newspaper clipping shows the Allied advanced party addressing
liberated internees at Chapei in August 1945. (Howard Allred)

with hardship, 13 of the non-licensed crew did not survive their internment in Shanghai.

Although causes, dates, and places of their deaths are not available for most, some information is available, at least with respect to ages. (Some are approximations derived from ages given on the original crew list.) Ten of the group were at least 50 years of age, and quite possibly had pre-existing health problems. For example, Odin Steen, the chief reefer engineer who died at Chapei at age 56, had a history of epilepsy. Max Miller, a German-born waiter, was known to be in marginal health before his stay in Shanghai where he died in his mid-50s. Several of the more senior men survived almost through the war, only to succumb at the last: John Spak, a quartermaster, died in Shanghai at age 41 just two days before the end of the war; and another quartermaster, 55-year-old Joseph Pierpont--the man who had been steering the ship when it hit the rocks at Shaweishan--died en route home aboard the hospital ship *Refuge* after he had been liberated.

The other near or post-50-year-olds who died in captivity were all in the steward's department where generally the physical standards were not as high as in the other departments. These included John Lentz, the night steward, and Edward Utz, storekeeper, each of whom died before confinement; Edward Diamond, bartender; Harry Newman, saloonman; James Wright, waiter; Henry Roberts, room steward; and Alfred Lee, chief baker. Utz was the oldest, about 65 when he died, and Wright was only a year younger.

The two other men who died in Shanghai, however, were relatively young. August Enos, a wiper, was only about 32, and laundryman Lui K. Young, who as Chinese had not been confined in any camp, was 30 when he died. One can only speculate about the fate of these two men.

For those who died the struggle was over, but, for the nine out of 10 who survived, the battle to sustain morale and spirit went on. It must have been discouraging to see the well-connected and affluent British and American residents of the camps draw support from their non-interned friends in the city while most of the *Harrison* crew lacked such contacts. Furthermore, crewmembers were given no indication that any of their efforts, enroute to Chinwangtao or in Shanghai, had been noticed or appreciated by anyone. Although they may not have been the forgotten men of World War II, they perhaps could have qualified as the least remembered group of civilians used by the Navy to further its military objectives in the war.

Those in the crew who emerged reasonably intact when liberation came in September 1945, could not be called *heroes* in the usual meaning of that term, certainly not in the same sense that Smith and Polkinghorn were. Instead, they had earned the more meaningful appellation of *survivors*, a term that suggests triumph against great odds in the psychological as well as physiological sense. In a quiet ongoing way they had prevailed over a long series of day-to-day crises in this unfamiliar setting where self-doubt was the biggest enemy to be overcome. The had shown themselves to be capable, resourceful, and resilient. These merchant mariners were indeed tough, as George Laycock had labelled them, but their toughness was built on durability and fortitude, not on two-fisted power. In this outpost of European privilege and class consciousness they showed a glimpse of the American melting pot in which room stewards could be entrepreneurs, pantrymen could be administrative assistants, and second stewards and second butchers could cater a large-scale internment lasting several years.

Just as their ship, the *President Harrison*, has done for so many years, these American seamen showed the flag well.

Chapter 9

The Ship as Captive

Ever since her grounding on Shaweishan Island the *President Harrison* had been a Japanese ship. From late January to early March 1942, she lay at the Jardine wharf at Shanghai, her crew still aboard while Japanese salvage workers continued to strengthen her patched-up hull. Even though the Japanese flag now flew over her, the large American flag was still painted on her hull, offering Americans in Shanghai their last opportunity to see the Stars and Stripes for the balance of the war.

The movements of the ship for the next two and a half years are difficult to reconstruct. Unlike the captured American naval vessels which were integrated into the Imperial Navy and were tracked by historians, the *Harrison* and the one other captured American merchant ship, the *Admiral Y. S. Williams*, apparently remained as merchant vessels, and thus achieved relative anonymity among historians. Their names were known--the *Williams* became the *Tasutama Maru* while the *Harrison* became in turn the *Kakko Maru* and the *Kachidoki Maru*--but their movements went largely unreported for the most part. Only signal events in their operations were recorded: surviving the war in the case of the *Williams* and not surviving the war in the case of the *Harrison*.

It seems reasonable to conclude that the Japanese did move the *Harrison* to complete her rehabilitation, sometime in the spring of 1942. Shanghai had shipyards, but the Japanese yards were better equipped to effect major repairs on ships the size of the 502s than were the local yards in China. She was obviously a fine prize and worthy of a first-rate reconstruction job. At the end of the war when losses to American submarines were tallied up, losses that left only 10 per cent of Japan's pre-war merchant fleet intact, it was evident that there had been only about 15 transports equal in size to or larger than the *Harrison* in that sunken fleet. Thus, the determination of the Japanese to capture the ship and put her back into service was logical and understandable.

It has been assumed that she was back in service no later than mid-1942, but no one seems to know the exact date. Stories persist that the *Harrison* was sunk by an American submarine on her first voyage in 1942, only to be salvaged and put back into service. Indeed, this legend represents another of the major mysteries of the *Harrison* saga, akin to that of Peking Man. The accounts of this reported sinking vary somewhat and tend to be fragmentary, but they contain enough common elements to suggest a germ of probability. Most of the references to such a sinking occurred in post-war sources, but at least two reports were made during 1944 and 1945.

Perhaps the original basis for the story was an interview by the *New York Times* with Clara G. Main, the stewardess from the *President Harrison*'s crew. This interview was published shortly after the *Gripsholm* brought the second load of repatriated Americans back to New York City in December 1943.

After a review of her own capture and internment, Mrs. Main announced to reporters that the *Harrison* had subsequently been sunk by an American submarine a short distance down the river from Shanghai while on her first voyage for the Japanese with a cargo of autos, trucks, and other equipment. The stewardess was quoted as saying, "Of course, that was only grapevine information, but we did receive the news of the sinking and there was very little information that came over the grapevine that didn't turn out to be true."

Shortly after the end of the war the *West Coast Sailor*, the newspaper of the Sailors' Union of the Pacific, reported in a story on the return of the crew of the ship that, "The *Harrison* was later sunk by an American sub as the Japs were moving her for repairs." Presumably, this information came from some of the returning members of the crew.

Rumors have interesting patterns of development. Mrs. Main's story included a specific cargo for the ship and a fairly specific location for her demise. The version which was brought home by the crew, while apparently deriving from the same source, was inherently more logical in its details, but still in error. For example, the crewmembers knew, at the time they went ashore in Shanghai, that the Japanese wanted to take the ship to Japan for further work. The crew's version also recognized tacitly the impossibility of a submarine torpedo attack in the Yangtze, inasmuch as ships could scarcely clear the bottom

120

on high tide while a submerged submarine was a physical impossibility in those waters.

How certain members of the crew developed their version of the sinking of the *Harrison* while they were in Shanghai is not easy to imagine. Possibly they listened to the same "grapevine" as had the stewardess to get the basic story. But if there indeed had been an early sinking the Japanese would not have been inclined to release such information. It is also unlikely that the U.S. Navy released information on the 1944 sinking of the *Kachidoki Maru* to the general public, although the *New York Times* acknowledged the loss in an item on its shipping page in November of that year, dealing with the fate of pre-war liners. Even less likely was the possibility that the crew of the *Harrison* would have had a chance to hear of this later confirmed sinking. At the time Mrs. Main left China in the summer of 1943 with the story, the verifiable sinking of the *Harrison* had not occurred. Possibly what she brought home was wishful thinking, while the crew may have later heard something about the 1944 sinking and connected it up with the earlier rumor.

Still later, in a 1952 story dealing with the disappearance of Peking Man, the *New York Times* reported that the *Harrison* had been sunk by an American submarine on her first voyage as a Japanese ship. By this time the newspaper should have known better. This story was given additional detail and authenticity when it appeared in the 1959 book, the *H. W. McCurdy Marine History of the Pacific Northwest*. In the chapter "Events of 1942" is this item: "The *Kachidoki Maru* had another close brush with disaster, being torpedoed by an American submarine after leaving Shanghai with a cargo of motor vehicles and other military supplies for the Japanese Army." At this point the item simply parroted the story of Mrs. Main which had been carried at the time in Seattle papers. Now a new dimension was added, as the book continued, "She was again salvaged, however, and returned to war service under the Rising Sun flag." The staff of the Puget Sound Maritime Historical Society, which furnished materials for the McCurdy history, cannot identify a specific source for this item, so it may be impossible to determine how the concept of salvaging the vessel entered the story.

But the strangest angle in the development of the story came out of the records kept on the *Harrison* by the San Francisco Marine Exchange which for decades had maintained a card on each vessel using the port. Appended to the *Harrison's* card was another page on which, following a cryptic reference to a quartermaster on the ship, was penned a comment on the fate of the *Harrison*, saying "She was sunk by the U.S. submarine *Steelhead* between Japan and the Philippines." Indeed, Navy records show that on July 10, 1943, the USS *Steelhead* fired 10 torpedoes at what she described as a Japanese task force. Explosions were heard, but damage to the targets could not be determined. While this story departs from the time frame of most of the others, it has a disturbing specificity that is difficult to refute.

Clearly, the possibility of a sinking in 1942 or 1943 cannot be ruled out. During that time in the East and South China Seas there were several sinkings by American submarines for which the Japanese have been unable to supply the names of the ships involved. In addition to the *Steelhead's* unconfirmed and unknown victim in June 1943, the *Gudgeon* was credited with both a cargo and passenger/cargo vessel in late March of 1942 between Japan and China, the *Seahorse* a cargo vessel in the same area in November 1943, and the *Haddock* a transport north of Formosa in August 1942. Four additional "unknown marus" were credited to submarines operating off the south coast of Japan: a cargo vessel by the *Drum* in May 1942, a cargo vessel by the *Pompano* in August 1942, and a cargo vessel and a transport by the *Silversides* in May and July of 1942. There was even a *Kokku Maru* sunk on August 1, 1943, off the China coast. In each case the estimated tonnage of the vessels sunk was significantly lower than that of the *Harrison*, but on these early patrols American submarine skippers had not yet acquired much experience in such tonnage assessments.

The issue of the additional sinking may, however, have finally been put to rest. At the request of the author, in 1988 the Defense Attache of the U.S. Embassy in Tokyo contacted the Japanese Maritime Institute, which is the research organization of the Ministry of Transport. The Institute found the 1944 sinking of the *Kachidoki Maru* listed in the *History of Japanese Merchant Marine Accidents*, but no reference to a 1942 or 1943 sinking. This information would seem to suggest strongly that the additional sinking did not take place, and that Clara Main's "grapevine" in Shanghai was not infallible.

One factor which had tended to support the possibility of

the *Harrison* being involved in the second sinking off the China coast was her presence in the area which had been verified in a widely-cited report. General Jonathan Wainwright said he saw the ship in August 1942, from the ship on which he was confined at Takao on the southwest coast of Formosa. In his book, *General Wainwright's Story*, another of the many ghost-written books about war experiences, the general says that, "Our ship came in through the canal and anchored just off the stern of the old *President Harrison* of the President Lines. The Japs has seized this fine American liner in the early days of the war after it went aground on one of the small islands below Formosa while trying to escape."

It is not clear how Wainwright recognized the *Harrison* by name. He may have been familiar with the 502s from his days in Manila where they called frequently, but it is unlikely that he could tell one from another. He may have been told about the capture of the ship before being captured himself, and simply surmised that this was the *Harrison* that he saw in Takao. He did not report her Japanese name at that time; knowing which name she bore would have been helpful in latter-day efforts to establish what happened to the ship in 1942 because the change from Kakko to Kachidoki might conceivably have reflected a major overhaul growing out of an incident of some kind. Inasmuch as Wainwright's book is not particularly strong on detail in other matters, it is hard to understand why seeing the *Harrison* was fixed so definitely in his mind, even down to the exact date of August 14, 1942. That date, incidentally, would have ruled out the possibility of the *Haddock* sinking the *Harrison* since her sinking of an unknown transport was on August 12th, which would have made it difficult for the ship to be floating serenely at Takao two days later.

Another significant sighting of the ship at the same time and place occurred when Carl and Shelley Mydans, photo-journalists for *Life* Magazine were being transported from Manila to Shanghai in September 1942, on the *Maya Maru* which must have been the same ship on which General Wainwright had been transported. In his book Wainwright used only the sobriquet *Stinko Maru* for this ship. The Mydans were ultimately repatriated on the second trip of the *Gripsholm*, bringing back an account which contradicted Clara Main. In a *Life* article late in 1943 they reported seeing the *President Harrison* in 1942

loading Japanese troops in Takao harbor crowded with transports forming into a large convoy. As with General Wainwright,
their account provided no clue as to how they knew that this
Japanese ship was the *Harrison*. Possibly other passengers
enroute from Manila to Takao or Shanghai were familiar with the
ship; if the seamen from the *President Grant* were aboard
enroute to Shanghai they may have been able to identify the
Harrison as a sister 502, although it is not clear whether the fate
of the latter ship would have been publicly known in Manila
during the first few weeks of the war before the *Grant* crew was
interned. In any case, the 1942 sighting of the *Harrison* was the
last reported sighting for two years. When she was next seen by
American eyes it was through the lens of a periscope.

When that happened, more than two and a half years had
passed since the *President Harrison*'s capture by the Japanese.
The war had gone reasonably well for her captors, but now in
the summer of 1944 the tide was turning and American forces
were gaining momentum in their drive northward. Saipan had
been taken, but as yet the Philippines were still in Japanese
hands. Freedom was yet a year away for the hundreds of
Americans whose captivity grew out of their being aboard, or
scheduled to be aboard, the *Harrison* during the China episodes.

The ship had long been in the service of her captors. She
probably had the status of a merchant ship inasmuch as she
does not appear in authoritative lists of Japanese warships, lists
which include both transports and captured ships. How long
she served as the *Kakko Maru* is unknown; it was as the
Kachidoki Maru that she was to earn her second niche in the
maritime history of World War II.

As the largest American ship to fall into enemy hands she
went singularly unnoticed by American intelligence officers. The
Navy should have been aware of her status; the first report of
her capture was made through her own radio messages, going
to the Navy among others, and in news stories originating with
the wire services. In February 1942, the Chief of Naval Operations reported to the Maritime Commission that the ship had
been salvaged and was then "docked in the Whangpoo River."
With the repatriation of the four men of the 4th Marines from
Shanghai in mid-1942 the status of the ship earlier in the year
should have been clear to the Navy. A year later that status
would have been reaffirmed by the next set of repatriated

civilians, including the *Life* journalists who were aware of her earlier location--unless, of course, the Navy accepted the story of a sinking in 1942 or 1943. In any case, the Navy should have known that the Japanese were using the ship extensively in September of 1942 when she was seen in Takao. Perhaps coast watchers and others engaged in reconnaisance did not recognize her as the former American liner for several reasons: the modified 502s looked like many other medium-sized passenger ships, particularly in grey paint, and merchant ships of the United States and Japan differed much less markedly than did naval vessels of the two countries.

In September of 1944 three American submarines in the South China Sea, working together as a wolfpack, unknowingly found the venerable 502-type transport as they came across a large Japanese convoy. The encounter was not accidental; intercepted and decoded radio messages had given the position and projected course of the convoy to the submarine force commander in Hawaii, Vice Admiral Charles A. Lockwood Jr. But these intercepted messages had provided little information about the nature of the convoy.

The convoy sailing northeastward from Singapore toward Japan was made up of 10 ships: four naval escorts, two tankers, two freighters, and the two transports, the 10,500-ton *Kachidoki Maru* and the 9,400-ton *Rakuyo Maru*. Even though she was the larger of the two transports, the ex-*President Harrison* carried fewer prisoners than the other: 900 British prisoners, soldiers who had survived two and a half years of captive labor building the infamous railway line to Burma, only to be sent to the Japanese homeland for further slave labor. The *Rakuyo Maru* carried a total of 1,318 prisoners, including 716 Australians, 599 Britishers, and a lone American, Colonel Harry Melton, an Air Corps pilot who had been shot down in Burma. On each transport several hundred wounded Japanese soldiers were also embarked, along with the medical personnel caring for them. But the Japanese had not asked for safe conduct for these ships as they had sometimes done for hospital ships or vessels with Red Cross cargo, so there was no way for the submarine commanders to know that there were prisoners of war and wounded aboard the two ships in the convoy. Since there was a partial cargo of rubber aboard each vessel, it would have been a violation of the rules of warfare if the Japanese had asked for

125

safe conduct for the ships.

Life aboard the transports was understandably miserable for the prisoners. Confined at night in the stifling holds and given very little food and water, the troops were in poor and deteriorating physical condition during the voyage. Tropical fever, dysentery, and the effects of dehydration and malnutrition ravaged the prisoners. The treatment by Japanese guards was harsh, although the prisoners detected a desire on the part of the guard commanders to get their human cargoes to Japan without excessive attrition. Conditions were somewhat better on the *Kachidoki Maru* than on the *Rakuyo Maru*, but prisoners on the latter ship showed more resourcefulness in adapting to their environment. Aided by navy personnel in their numbers who were survivors of the Australian cruiser *Perth* which had been sunk in 1942, the officer prisoners of the *Rakuyo Maru* actually organized an abandon ship plan which included provisions for releasing all buoyant equipment topside.

On the *Kachidoki Maru*, during their hours topside in pursuit of fresh air, the prisoners had noticed the ship's bell with the name *President Harrison* on it. They were naturally curious and there was speculation as to why that name should appear on a Japanese ship, but the prisoners knew no more about the ship's past than they did about her future.

For most of the trip the weather was hot and clear, but on September 10th a refreshing rain fell. Those prisoners with canteens were able to fill them, and to enjoy ample water for the first time. On the 11th of September six additional ships from Manila joined the convoy: three freighters and three escorts. The convoy was now in the middle of the South China Sea, beyond the protection of land-based aircraft. In the early hours of the next morning the 16 ships in three columns steaming at 11 knots reached the point where the three American submarines were waiting.

These submarines were a mixed lot. The USS *Growler* with the wolfpack command embarked was a seasoned veteran with an outstanding war record. The USS *Sealion*, although quite new, had already put together a fine record. She was the second World War II boat to carry the name; the first had been damaged in the initial Japanese bombing of the Cavite Naval Station at Manila, and had to be blown up by Navy personnel to prevent her from falling into Japanese hands. The third boat,

Smaller than the *Kachidoki Maru*, the *Rakuyo Maru* still carried more Allied POWs than did the former *President Harrison*. (Steamship Historical Society of America)

The *Pampanito* sank the *Kachidoki Maru*, not knowing that her victim was the former *President Harrison* and that she was loaded with Allied POWs. (National Maritime Museum)

The survivors of the *Rakuyo Maru* were oily and begrimed when they were picked up by the *Pampanito*. (National Maritime Museum Association)

The captain of the *Pampanito*, Commander Paul Summers, earned the Navy Cross for the rescue of the survivors of the *Rakuyo Maru*. (National Maritime Museum Association)

The routes of the convoy and the *Pampanito* are shown on this map of the South China Sea. (National Maritime Museum Association)

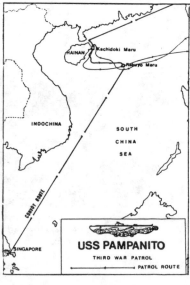

USS *Pampanito*, as we shall see shortly, was something of a nonentity within the submarine force.

The *Growler* began the attack at about 1:30 a.m. within a successful surface torpedo run which quickly sank the largest escort vessel, a destroyer. In the resultant confusion ships in the convoy took evasive action in all directions. The *Kachidoki Maru* and a tanker actually collided in a glancing bow-on encounter that produced dents and scratches, but miraculously neither ship was seriously damaged. The escorts were able to drive off the attacking submarines for the time being, and the convoy regrouped, swinging sharply to the west toward the island of Hainan off the coast of China.

Three hours later the *Sealion* maneuvered in closely for another surface attack. In quick succession she was able to sink a tanker and a freighter. Both of these ships blazed brightly, illuminating the scene for still a third sinking. This time the victim was the *Rakuyo Maru*. Two torpedoes, fired from only 1,100 yards and showing a wake visible to all on deck, slammed into the ship fore and aft. She settled in the water and began to sink.

Already in just a few hours the wolfpack had been highly successful. However, the third submarine, the *Pampanito*, had not contributed. Instead she had done everything wrong, guessing incorrectly about the convoy's intentions and going east when the targets had gone west. She had not fired a single torpedo, bearing out her nickname throughout the fleet as "The Peaceful Pamp." Perhaps she had been given a bad rap, but it was no secret that both the submarine and her skipper, 31-year-old Commander Paul E. Summers, were regarded as being overly cautious. As the *Pampanito* continued to miss out completely on the turkey shoot that was going on around her--and unbeknownst to her--that reputation seemed fully justified.

But Summers persisted. He headed west, hoping to overtake the convoy. In mid-day he picked up a smudge of smoke on the horizon. After dark he lost contact, but luckily found the convoy again on radar, only about 50 miles off Hainan. Working his way ahead of the remaining ships, he planned to fire a spread of 10 torpedoes, but a jam in one tube forced him to go with only nine instead. Cautious as always, he fired from the maximum effective range, almost 4,000 yards, in a surface attack with no moonlight. This time he had luck on his side; he scored two sets of fatal hits, one on a freighter and the other on the *Kachidoki Maru*.

Unlike the *Rakuyo Maru* which had taken many hours to sink, permitting all the prisoners to abandon ship, the *Kachidoki Maru* went down quickly. Paradoxically, the prisoners on the second torpedoed ship were slow to realize the ship had been hit. Only a few were topside at the time; they witnessed the pandemonium among the Japanese crew, and knew that the ship was going to sink. The ship's captain shot himself; other officers shot wounded Japanese soldiers in the #3 hold. But when the POWs tried to rouse their shipmates below deck they could convince only a few that they should come on deck immediately. Five precious minutes were lost without any real movement of men up the ladders, and the ship was to stay afloat for only another 10 minutes. Finally, when the bow of the ship began to rise sharply the danger was apparent to everyone. By then it was too late; possibly a third of the prisoners never got away. The rest abandoned ship, using lifejackets which had been discovered earlier in one of the holds of the ship--perhaps the extra life-jackets left over from the Marine evacuation from Shanghai. At 11 o'clock at night, the *Kachidoki Maru*, ex-*President Harrison*, slid stern first into the sea in 360 feet of water, just four days short of the 24th anniversary of her launching.

Captain Summers on the *Pampanito*, of course, had no way of knowing that he had sunk a ship full of prisoners of war. He did not even know what ship he had sunk. In his action report he described the target only as a "large transport" or "large AP." American submarine commanders often could find pictures of their potential targets in recognition manuals which they had in front of them as they made their approaches. The *Pampanito*, however, seems to have had no such picture or silhouette of the *Kachidoki Maru* available for this purpose. A month would pass before the identity of the sunken ship was officially established.

Summers broke off the engagement long enough to reload his tubes, then moved in for another attack. This time he fired three torpedoes from 3,500 yards at an escort vessel which appeared to be picking up survivors, but all shots missed. He withdrew from the action permanently, his crew disgruntled at this lack of aggressiveness.

128

The *Pampanito* stayed off the coast of Hainan for the next two days, submerged during daylight hours to escape detection by land-based aircraft. Captain Summers was unaware that a rescue drama was being played out around him. Fortunately for the men in the water the Japanese guards on the *Kachidoki Maru* were more concerned about recovering their prisoners than were those on the *Rakuyo Maru*. During the day after the sinking two frigates and a trawler crisscrossed the area busily plucking survivors from the water. After they had recovered 520 British prisoners and a large number of their own wounded troops these three vessels headed for Hainan.

Using a high periscope scan during daylight hours Summers saw only a single lifeboat which apparently had men in it-- probably prisoner survivors since the Japanese had picked up their own personnel first--but he assumed they were Japanese since he had no reason to think otherwise. He also saw smoke which may have been coming from the three small vessels enroute to Hainan with the recaptured prisoners, but he decided not to investigate, a fortunate decision for the *Kachidoki Maru* survivors who were certainly in no shape to endure another sinking.

Eventually the *Pampanito* gave up the hunt. By this time the remnants of the convoy had probably reached Hainan, so the submarine headed east to rendezvous with the rest of the wolfpack which had been operating independently. On her way back, near the scene of the initial attack three nights earlier, the *Pampanito* stumbled across the evidence of the *Rakuyo Maru* sinking, thus setting in motion the final act of this strange drama.

Late in the afternoon of September 15th the *Pampanito* came upon debris in the water, followed by two makeshift life rafts. Approaching warily, Captain Summers saw that there were men aboard the rafts. Because they were so dark and begrimed, he could not determine their ethnicity or nationality until he heard shouting in English. On a close pass he told his crew to pick up only one man for interrogation. Once aboard, that man, an Australian named Frank Farmer, explained that they were Australian and British survivors of the *Rakuyo Maru*, and that the sea around them was full of others. Whether he also reported that there had been a second ship in the convoy with prisoners of war was not made clear in the *Pampanito*'s action report.

Aware for the first time of what had happened, Summers radioed Commander, Submarine Force, Pacific, in Hawaii the news that possibly a large number of men were in the water at the scene of the *Rakuyo Maru* sinking. The *Pampanito* was soon joined by the *Sealion* in a massive rescue effort which succeeded in pulling 127 survivors from the sea, 73 by the *Pampanito* and 54 by the *Sealion*. Exhausted, covered with oil, and wearing little clothing to protect them from the elements, these men were brought aboard assisted by swimmers in the water and eager hands on deck.

The rescued men described vividly their three-day ordeal in the water--battling with Japanese for pieces of debris, seeing friends hallucinate and die, losing contact with large groups of shipmates who drifted away, even hearing bursts of machine-gun fire as Japanese ships combed the area. They recounted moments of heroism as well as moments of savagery, and even of national pride when the strains of "Rule Britannia" and "There'll Always Be an England" could be heard coming from the voices of scores of men struggling in the water.

Later two additional submarines were ordered into the search, the *Queenfish* which rescued 18 men and the *Barb* which found 14. The four submarines then proceeded independently back to Saipan 1,800 miles away. During the long and crowded trip seven men died, one aboard *Pampanito*, four on the *Sealion*, and two on the *Queenfish*.

During the passage to Saipan enlisted medical personnel aboard the submarines performed incredible feats of stamina and the healing arts in insuring that the survivors were given the best possible chance of recovery. Members of each crew cheerfully gave up their bunks to the survivors who were made to feel as shipmates, not outsiders.

Admiral Lockwood was so pleased with the sacrifice and dedication displayed by his crews that he initiated a quick round of decorations and promotions for a number of the key personnel. Captain Summers, along with the other wolfpack skippers, was awarded the Navy Cross. More important, the *Pampanito*'s tarnished image was restored. "The Peaceful Pamp," if not the best at sinking Japanese shipping, was now at least the champion of humanitarian rescue.

It was only at this time that the identity of the *Kachidoki Maru* was established. Apparently the survivors of the *Rakuyo*

130

Maru, if they mentioned the second transport at all, had not provided her name to Captain Summers. The *Pampanito's* Report of War Patrol Three, describing the sinking of a "large AP," was addressed to Commander-in-Chief, U.S. Fleet, via four intermediate commands. It went first to Commander, Submarine Division 202, whose endorsement added no new information. The second endorsement was by Commander, Submarine Squadron Nine, who recommended that the *Pampanito* be given credit for three ships, including one AP of 10,500 tons, "similar to the *Kokoku Maru*." Actually, the *Kokoku Maru* was a 544-ton vessel sunk early in the war. What the squadron commander had in mind may have been the *Kokuyo Maru* of 10,027 tons or the *Hokoku Maru* of 10,439 tons. The latter ship was one of the surface raiders that had captured the crews of the *Vincent* and *Malama* at the beginning of the war, only to be sunk in turn in November 1942, in a battle with an Indian minesweeper and a Dutch tanker. Or could the listing for *Kokoku Maru* conceivably have been a garbled version of the *Kakko Maru*, the first Japanese name of the *Harrison*, from an American intelligence document?

On the third endorsement to the *Pampanito's* report, that of Commander Submarine Force, Pacific Fleet, dated 12 October 1944, the large AP was finally identified as the *President Harrison*; the name *Kachidoki Maru* does not appear in this correspondence. This date apparently marks the first official recognition that the former American liner had been sunk.

It was not until the war ended that the final calculations could be made, still in the form of estimates, on the death toll from the sinking of the two ships. It appeared that of the 1,325 men on the *Rakuyo Maru* less than 300 survived: 159 picked up by the American submarines and 136 picked up by the Japanese escorts. On the *Kachidoki Maru* 520 of the 900 aboard had survived the sinking.

All the *Rakuyo Maru* survivors picked up by the Japanese were taken to Hainan where they had a brief reunion with the survivors from the other transport. Those from the *Rakuyo Maru* had been given decent treatment aboard the escorts en route to Hainan, and were in better shape physically and psychologically than their counterparts from the *Kachidoki Maru*, who seemed utterly demoralized by the experience. After first indicating their intention of taking the more than 600 prisoners to Japan as deck passengers on a tanker, the Japanese gave in to the protests of officer prisoners and provided instead a whale factory ship, the *Kibibi Maru*. On September 16, 1944, just four days after the attack on the prison ship convoy, this ship sailed for Japan with the Allied prisoners and about 1,000 Japanese survivors of the convoy. After a difficult trip the prisoners eventually reached Japan, but some did not survive the war as Allied bombs fell on prison camps there during subsequent air raids.

Because of the wide dispersal of the prisoners and the continuing deaths among their ranks from bombings as well as from the privations of captivity, a final tally of how many of the *Rakuyo Maru* and *Kachidoki Maru* prisoners survived the war has been impossible. It is unlikely, however, that any of the 1,562 men who were not picked up by the American submarines or the Japanese escort vessels later turned up alive. Included in this group of missing in action and presumed dead was the American pilot, Colonel Melton.

Other prison ships, including several loaded with Americans, were sunk at about the same time, making the recollection of this entire period of submarine warfare against the Japanese rather unpleasant for submariners and ex-POWs alike. At least six Japanese merchant vessels with American and Allied prisoners of war on board were sunk by American submarines and planes during the last year of the war; several other sinkings had occurred earlier. During the autumn of 1944 alone, over 4,000 Allied prisoners were killed or drowned aboard ships sunk by American submarines, including 1,765 from the *Arisan Maru*. Aircraft were also responsible for sinking other ships heavily loaded with prisoners; 1,058 Americans were lost in a two-day carrier aircraft assault on the *Oryku Maru* at Subic Bay, plus 31 more casualties resulting from the sinking of the *Enoura Maru* which had rescued survivors of the *Oryku Maru*. One estimate puts the number of men of the 4th Marines killed in submarine and air attacks on prisoner ships at 184.

These sinkings raise the questions, how much did submarine or aircraft commanders know about the ships they stalked, and how much could they have known if better dissemination of intelligence had occurred? Inasmuch as the convoy in which the *Kachidoki Maru* was sunk had originated in Singapore, the great British Crown Colony, it seems likely that some kind of underground organization or intelligence agency must have existed there in 1944 which could have provided information that the two transports had loaded over 2,000 Allied prisoners. It also seems reasonable that in six days time this information could have been disseminated from Pearl Harbor to fleet boats in the western Pacific.

Unfortunately, by its very nature the intelligence establishment cannot "go public" with much of its former activities, although a number of the smashing successes of World War II were well publicized. Thus, it is unlikely that we will ever learn whether the sinking of the *Kachidoki Maru*, *Rakuyo Maru*, and the other "hell ships" might have been averted.

Often overlooked amidst the ambivalent feelings about these infamous sinkings is the most deplorable story of all--that of the *President Harrison*, full of heroism, irony, futility, and tragedy. Unlike the *Rakuyo Maru* whose prisoners at least had the chance to battle for survival with their captors as well as with the sea itself, the *Harrison* was unable to grant any real freedom to her captives, even the transitory and perilous freedom of bobbing alone as men against the sea. Furthermore, lost in the regrets over the sinking of the *Kachidoki Maru* is the distressing reality that she would never have been a Japanese prison ship if the American Navy had exercised better judgment in trying to rescue 200 Marines from North China in 1941.

The only existing memorial to the SS *President Harrison* is the first of six Japanese merchant ensigns representing the ships sunk by the *Pampanito*, appearing on the battle flag of the submarine at the National Maritime Museum, San Francisco. (National Maritime Museum Association)

Chapter 10

The Aftermath

For the crew of the *Harrison* the war had begun suddenly, dramatically, decisively. It ended with the kind of waiting, confusion, and indecision that has become synonomous with the collapse of a governmental regime.

The atomic bombs were dropped on Hiroshima and Nagasaki on August 6th and 9th, respectively. On the 10th the Japanese government issued a statement indicating its willingness to surrender. Emperor Hirohito on August 15th in a broadcast to his subjects at home and overseas announced that the nation would accept the surrender terms of the Allies.

One of those terms was that the Japanese would furnish a list of the names, locations, and populations of all POW camps, and that such camps would be clearly marked. The first such list, available on August 27th, contained a total of 73 camps. In a series of reconnaisance flights American forces verified the existence and location of 57 additional camps, and ultimately air drops of food and supplies were made at a total of 158 POW and civilian internment camps in the Far East.

Although Shanghai was not a major sector of the war which could expect a large number of occupying troops, events initially moved relatively quickly toward freedom for the internees around the city, faster than for the POWs who had been moved to the north. A leaflet was dropped into camps on August 12th, indicating the end was near and asking everyone to remain in camp. Within a few days after the Emperor's message the Japanese commandants and guards quietly vanished from the camps, in some cases taking internees' passports with them. After another few days, on about August 22nd, the first American representatives arrived at Pootung and Chapei in the form of several junior officers from the Army and Navy who were part of liberation teams. The bulk of American forces did not reach Shanghai for several weeks when a port director's group came upriver under the command of Columbus D. Smith, the former skipper of the *Wake*, now a captain in the Navy. For all practical purposes the internees were now free, but now they would have to wait for logistics to catch up with liberation. A month would pass before they could start home.

Most of the crew stayed in camp during this waiting period, fattening up on the food parcels parachuted in by American planes and getting organized for the trip home, as well as protecting their belongings from Chinese looters. But a few curious people ventured into Shanghai to see what was happening in the city. One who did was the fireman, Gil Monreal, who managed to stumble into an adventure out of a James Bond film. In a restaurant he was approached by the agent of a rich Chinese patron who wanted to show his appreciation for Americans by hosting a group of them. Monreal and two friends from Lungwha agreed to meet the man, and were whisked off in a bullet-proof limousine accompanied by two men with sub-machine-guns to a large steel-doored compound in the International Settlement. Here the Chinese benefactor explained that he and his men were part of the Chinese underground, now engaged in tracking down and disposing of collaborators. After toasting the United States and China, he invited his guests to make use of an adjacent apartment house which was staffed with a cook and houseboy and supplied with ample stocks of food and liquor. This man may have been Tu Yueh Sun, pre-war opium king and gangster of the French Concession, who was both the head of a secret society and a crony of Chaing Kai Shek. Monreal spent a number of days in this opulent life style, and at the invitation of the patron invited others from Lungwha to participate in the good life. Only the pending repatriation and a desire to see all his camp friends again brought him back to Lungwha and away from this strange and exotic taste of the hidden side of life in Shanghai. As noted previously, if anyone in the Orient *had* to be a captive in World War II, Shanghai was certainly the place to be one.

Farther north, the Allied command had to assemble a large enough occupation force to go ashore in the potentially dangerous Japanese home islands and in the nearby areas of Korea and Manchuria. The advance party arrived in Japan on the 28th of August. Prisoner releases began immediately, and as tens of thousands of American troops swarmed ashore during the next several weeks, the pace of liberation stepped up. The first combat troops, symbolically the 4th Marines, came ashore on the

30th, led by Brigadier General William T. Clement who had been on Admiral Hart's staff in Manila four years earlier. The formal surrender was signed aboard the USS *Missouri* on September 2, 1945. On the 9th of the month Captain Pierson of the *Harrison* was liberated from the Roko Roshi camp. Other *Harrison* officers followed, but in some cases they spent as much as a month in camp before they could start home.

The officers were generally provided air or ship transportation individually to mustering centers in Okinawa or the Philippines from which they were flown home as quickly as space was available. One exception was Chief Engineer Joseph C. "Shaky" Smith, who was so anxious to get back to sea that he signed on the *Cape Sanders* in Manila in October.

The unlicensed personnel of the *Harrison* boarded the Navy hospital ship *Refuge* in Shanghai on September 27, 1945, for a short trip to Okinawa where they were to be assigned to another ship for the trip home to San Francisco. Even with her naval modifications the *Refuge* looked familiar to the crew. She was, of course, the old *President Madison*, the sister ship 502 which had been with the *Harrison* almost four years earlier at Shanghai. At Okinawa the crew boarded the USS *Sanctuary*, a C4-type hospital ship for the trans-Pacific crossing. On October 13th she crossed the International Date Line which marked the war zone the crew had entered westbound on the *Harrison* on October 28, 1941. After a stop in Honolulu, where the Hawaiian crewmembers left the ship, the *Sanctuary* went on to San Francisco, passing under the Golden Gate Bridge on October 22, four years and five days after the crew had last seen this impressive symbol of American ties to the Pacific.

In making their return crossing the *Harrison* crew was apparently given priority over certain other released prisoners. For example, the crew of the Matson ship *Malama*, who had been imprisoned as long as had the *Harrison* crew, was assembled in Manila, but forced by the Army to compete with military personnel possessing a large number of "points" earned under the formula by which the priorities of the "Magic Carpet" homeward trooplift were determined. When the captain of the *Cape Meares*, an Army-allocated and Matson-operated C1-type troop ship, learned that the *Malama* crew had not been cleared by the Transportation Corps for return passage on his vessel, he found space for them aboard, and departed Manila with his unauthorized repatriates. The *Harrison* crew, fortunately, encountered no such red tape.

It is impossible to know what happened to all the surviving members of the *Harrison*'s crew upon their return to the United States. After a period of rest and rehabilitation a number of them went back to sea; others had had enough, and went ashore permanently. As before, they lived their lives as individuals, with no bond of kinship as a unique group--the crew. Unlike the 200 men of the North China Marines or the larger group of 4th Marines who have frequent reunions and a newsletter, the crewmembers of the *Harrison* have never gotten together to reminisce. A few stay in touch with each other as friends, but for the most part they have chosen to forget the common experience that once brought them all together. Because of their limited contact with each other, only about a dozen surviving crewmembers could be located during the research for this book, two of whom died after initial contacts had been established.

After the war the crewmembers were united on one occasion, but it was only on paper, when virtually all of them were litigants in a number of legal actions brought against American President Lines. Safely back in the States with the war over the crewmembers had looked forward to the one benefit of their long internment: drawing the back pay they had accumulated on the books. But as they counted this pay they discovered that the company had not paid them the full amount of the war zone bonus. The amounts paid covered only the time in 1941 between crossing the 180th meridian westbound until they reached Shanghai, and in 1945 after they left Shanghai until they crossed the 180th meridian eastbound; in other words, there was no pay for the three and a half years in Shanghai. The company took the position that the members of the crew should not receive the bonus for being on a ship in the war zone when they were not aboard a ship.

With more than $600,000 at stake, various groups of crewmembers through their unions then sued American President Lines in an effort to get the bonus payments for the full period of their internment. Crews from other ships such as the *Vincent, Malama,* and *Admiral Y. S. Williams* were also forced to go to court to seek their war bonuses. In each case the attorneys for the seamen first had to overcome a ruling by the

At the end of the war Captain Pierson of the *Harrison* was liberated from the Roko Roshi camp on Honshu. (Army Signal Corps)

The crew of the *Harrison* left China on the USS *Refuge* which, as the *President Madison*, had shared in the evacuation of the Shanghai Marines. (U.S. Naval Institute)

Official Organ, Sailors' Union of the Pacific

SEAFARERS INTERNATIONAL UNION

West Coast Sailors

SECURITY UNITY PROGRESS

VOLUME IX   SAN FRANCISCO, CALIF., FRIDAY, OCTOBER, 26, 1945   No. 8

HARRISON CREW BACK

Name of the former deck crew of the PRESIDENT HARRISON as photographed on board the hospital ship SANCTUARY shortly after arrival in San Francisco, Monday.

Reading left to right: First row: MATHEW MASKELL, A. B.; WILLIAM HARDING, A. B.; and HOWARD ALLRED, A. B.

Second row: ALFRED EGGAN, A. B.; CHESTER PIEKOS, A. B.; ALFRED MORDEN, A. B., and A. MORTENSEN, Carpenter.

Last row: R. BEHRENS, O. S.; C. ZACZIKIEWICX, A. B.; J. AGNEW, O. S.; C. MAROIS, A. B.; L. GRUSZECZKA, Qm.; JACKSON HARRIS, O. S. and THEODORE HOWARD, A. B.

Story On Page Six

The newspaper of the Sailors Union of the Pacific carried this picture of a number of deck department men of the *Harrison* on their arrival home. (Howard Allred)

Maritime War Emergency Board, a federal agency created in February 1942, to handle matters of equity and rights for seamen. This board determined that bonuses would not be paid for time spent ashore, and it made the ruling retroactive to December 7, 1941. A long-established feature of American maritime law also worked against the crew: the concept that shipping articles, as an employment contract, are terminated upon a shipwreck of the vessel.

The *Harrison* cases were brought in the names of three individuals: John Griffin, the third assistant engineer, for the officers represented by the Marine Engineers Beneficial Association and by the Masters, Mates, and Pilots; James Agnew, an ordinary seaman, for the unlicensed personnel of the deck and engine departments represented by the Sailors' Union of the Pacific and the Marine Firemen, Oilers, Watertenders, and Wipers Association; and August Federer, a bathroom steward, for a group of steward's department personnel represented by the Marine Cooks and Stewards Association. Another group of steward's department people was added later to the list of litigants. The cases were heard in 1947 in the United States District Court for the Northern California District, Southern Division. The cases were heard separately, but were consolidated for the purposes of a decision since the issues were identical in each case. The federal government entered the proceedings on the side of the company.

The outcome of the legal struggle was a masterpiece of semantic nitpicking. The district court cited the precedent in the administrative ruling by the Maritime War Emergency Board; it further held that the original riders to the shipping articles were ambiguous because they indicated that the war bonus "shall be paid while employees are in the war zone defined herein" without a specific definition of the zone. The only reference in the riders to applicable territory was a statement that the bonus would apply "from crossing of the 180th Meridian westbound until crossing the 180th Meridian eastbound." The court held that this wording did not constitute a definition of a war zone.

The court took the position that the ambiguity could best be resolved by applying a broader collective bargaining agreement then in effect between the unions and the steamship company to determine the intent of the ambiguous language. That agreement authorized payment of basic and emergency wages during internment, and the payment of war bonuses "while employees are in the war zones defined herein." This agreement went on to spell out the five war zones, including Zone III covering the China coast, each of which was described at the end of the phrase "voyages to..." The court ruled that no voyage could occur on land; therefore, no war bonuses were authorized for time spent in internment. Thus, the action by the seamen of the *Harrison* was denied.

Two years later the cases were considered again by the United States Court of Appeals, Ninth Circuit. This court ruled that the finding of the lower court was in error. Noting that the zone was essentially geographical and did not change with the coming and going of the crew, the ship, or the voyage, it held that the key paragraph of the rider to the articles should be construed as follows:

> *This [war bonus or] emergency wage increase [payable to the sailors under paragraph 3 and 4] to apply [in the war zone existing] from the [sailors'] crossing of the 180th Meridian westbound until [their] crossing of the 180th Meridian eastbound.*

With this reversal of the lower court, the crewmembers could finally get their war bonuses. A few others were later to get similar benefits, including the staff officers (pursers and doctor), and trustees for deceased and incompetent crewmembers. They were all soon to discover, however, that legal fees had eaten deeply into their long-anticipated nest-eggs.

Individual members of the *Harrison* could also apply for benefits under another program of restitution, the War Claims Act of 1948 which provided compensation for several categories of former prisoners and internees. Military prisoners of war could receive for each day of captivity $1.00 if their rations were substandard, and $1.50 if the provisions of the Geneva Convention of 1929 had not been followed. American civilians captured in American territory such as the Philippines, Guam, and Wake Island could receive $60 a month for their time as internees. It was under this provision that merchant seamen were originally eligible for restitution; a clause including time "in transit to or from such place" covered those seamen captured while serving on vessels operating near these possessions. The *Harrison's* crew qualified by virtue of having sailed from Manila to Chinwangtao, but their fellow American internees in the Shanghai camps generally did not qualify.

In 1954 a section authorizing payment specifically to merchant seamen was added to the law. This addition was apparently necessary to cover captured merchant seamen whose ships were not operating near these American territories, including those seamen captured by the Germans as well as those captured by the Japanese in non-American locations such as the crew of the *Admiral Y. S. Williams*, a ship that was in a drydock in Hong Kong when seized.

In both the original legislation and in the 1954 amendments citizenship was a requirement for eligibility. Thus, 11 of the *Harrison's* crew were not eligible to receive payment under the War Claims Act. Total payment for each crewmember for the 45 months of captivity amounted to $2,700 for which each person had to file an application. On this basis, it is unlikely that the entire crew benefitted from this federal restitution program to the same degree that it had benefitted from the legal cases against the company.

While American President Lines had lost the legal action brought by the crew, it was the federal government, of course, as the owner of the company that paid the seamen after the settlement. The government was pleased with the company's performance during the war years; APL had prospered, and was now healthy enough to look attractive again to private investors. As John Niven observes in his history of the company,

> APL had performed admirably under the extreme pressures of World War II. Although operations had been profitable there had been no excessive salaries and no systematic draining of assets as in the days of the Dollars. The results had been clear and positive: The shipping line was free of debt in 1945, its planning well advanced for the resumption of its traditional trade routes with new and improved carriers for peacetime commerce.

Even though the Maritime Commission wanted to get the company back into private ownership, it was in a position to

141

take ample time to line up the best possible deal. As it turned out, however, the transfer to private ownership would not be consumated until seven years after the end of the war, due to a complicated legal action brought by the company's one-time owners, the Dollar family.

The Dollars sued to regain control of the company, arguing that they had pledged their stock in the company as collateral against the debts, and since the company was now debt-free it should be returned to them. The Maritime Commission took the position that the company had been surrendered to the United States as creditor, in return for the Dollar family being released from any further liability. The Dollar legal team for a while was extremely successful in pushing its case, even getting an injunction requiring that the company stock be delivered to the family. But President Harry Truman intervened and issued a directive that the government's right to the stock be defended through all appropriate action. Eventually, following legal intervention by minority stockholders in San Francisco, largely bankers who were horrified at the thought of the company returning to the Dollars, a federal appeals court in California stayed the injunction.

Finally, a compromise was worked out. The stock would be sold publicly, with the proceeds being split evenly by the federal government and the Dollars. Under this arrangement the Dollars were also allowed to bid for the company. They bid the minimum acceptable bid of $14,000,000 while Matson bid $16,426,000 and the winning bid of $18,360,000 was made by APL Associates, a group of West Coast oilmen. The company was once again in private hands.

Following the war the American President Lines returned to the China trade with a new fleet of liners that included no 502s or 535s. For several years commerce flourished, but it became increasingly clear that China was headed for a major internal crisis. Before the entire country fell to the communists in 1949 another exodus of westerners had begun, and the last APL ships left Shanghai amid an atmosphere of impending peril akin to that experienced in 1941 when the *President Harrison* and *President Madison* made the final departures from Shanghai.

After the communist takeover China changed enormously from the days of the 4th Marines in Shanghai. Many of the changes made by the communists have distressed those Americans who were fond of the country, but in recent years the more open attitude of the government there toward the West suggests that some of the more positive influences of the old order may reappear in time. No American in good conscience can lament the passing of extraterritoriality, that unique system of foreign sovereignty in China, but old China hands can still reflect sentimentally on the cosmopolitan and affluent world that the system produced in Shanghai--even though it was all a thin facade over a life of provincialism and poverty for millions of Chinese.

The physical geography of the China coast has not changed in the ensuing years, but the place names have. Understandably, the rulers of communist China wanted to eliminate all traces of foreign domination in China, so the familiar street names of Shanghai--the Bund, Bubbling Well Road, Avenue Joffre--have all been changed to Chinese names. Similarly, those offshore islands with the interesting names--The Saddles, Gutzlaff, Bonham, the Rugged Islands, the Steep Islands--now bear Chinese names. Although Shaweishan required no new name, all references to the island inexplicably have been dropped from the *Coast Pilot*, inferring that mariners no longer need make use of it today in entering the Yangtze River from any direction.

Modern charts show the island to be four miles inside the ten meter depth curve. As a result of the extensive silting which has occurred during the ensuing years, the always marginal North Channel into the river has been abandoned. Depths west of the island where the *Harrison* came to rest are now four or five meters, 13 to 16 feet, suggesting that, even if the water were somewhat deeper in 1941, reaching the island to hit it was a remarkable accomplishment for a large ship drawing 15 to 18 feet when completely light. Perhaps the island is omitted today from the *Coast Pilot* because no responsible navigator aboard a large ship would come near to it. But a hazard is still a hazard; as the largest and most inshore island in the Yangtze delta, Shaweishan cannot be written out of the geography of China, even though her role in history could conceivably be ignored.

Historians do ignore those things that do not interest them. The *President Harrison* has never been singled out for any true recognition as the largest American ship captured during World War II, or as the only passenger liner so captured and used by the enemy. This is not to say that her name is forgotten. Indeed, in keeping with American President Lines policy the name *President Harrison* was used again. Between 1949 and 1964 it was assigned to a C3-type ship which APL then sold to Waterman Steamship, and again from 1966 to 1979 it was assigned to a C6 container ship which was ultimately traded in on a new container ship. Today there is no *President Harrison* in the APL fleet, but the name is kept alive by a geographical coincidence; when the company moved its corporate headquarters from San Francisco to Oakland in the early 1970s, the address for the company became 1800 Harrison Street.

As with APL, the war had been essentially kind to the people of the *Harrison* and to most of the other Americans involved in her story. Captain Pierson returned to command passenger liners of the American President Lines for many years, eventually becoming commodore of the fleet before his retirement. At this writing he is living in Tiburon, California, overlooking San Pablo Bay. At least two of his officers also commanded ships of APL in post-war years: John Saxton and Jon Thuesen. Captain Valdemar Nielsen of the *President Madison* had a later career similar to that of Captain Pierson in that he, too, commanded other APL passenger ships before becoming the commodore of the line. He, too, survives, living in Healdsburg, an hour's drive north of San Francisco.

The military personnel associated with the *Harrison*'s adventures in China also achieved success. Colonel Samuel L. Howard of the 4th Marines was promoted after the war to Major General, and went to North China as head of a Marine division occupying that area, finally retiring as a Lieutenant General. Colonel William Ashurst of the North China Marines, his health broken, stayed on for a few years in non-demanding staff positions in the Corps, but died in 1952 at age 59. Dr. William T. Foley, the Navy doctor for the North China Marines, returned to New York City where he remains today, a world-renowned cardiologist.

Also on the Navy side, Admiral Thomas Hart, who had seen his power and prestige erode early in the war, spent a quiet twilight tour on the General Board of the Navy during the war and then retired, later to serve briefly in the United States Senate. William A. Glassford, whose relationship to Admiral Hart reportedly had been more of a rival than a protege, after three successive retreats corresponding to the withdrawal and collapse of the Asiatic Fleet, was brought home and promoted to Vice

Admiral; he subsequently served as a diplomat in North Africa, and later in the war returned to active duty to hold a major command in Europe before retiring shortly after the war. Paul E. Summers of the *Pampanito* retired from the post-war Navy as a Rear Admiral.

The ships whose track-lines had crossed those of the *Harrison* had mixed success in their further careers. Some were not as lucky as were the men whose lives were touched by the *Harrison*. The USS *Wake* had become the *Tatara* for the Japanese; she was acquired as the *Tai Yuan* by the Chinese Nationalists after the war, and later by the communists. Her final fate is unknown. The *Harrison*'s nemesis from December 8th, the *Nagasaki Maru*, had been sunk by a mine at Nagasaki in May 1942; her captain, Genzaburo Suga, committed harakiri on the bridge as the ship was sinking. The *Idzumo*, the Japanese cruiser in Shanghai, whose guns had been trained on the *Wake*, the *Peterel*, and the *Conte Verde*, was sunk by American planes in Japanese waters late in the war.

Other ships were more fortunate. The *President Madison* survived the war with dignity, and was scrapped at Vancouver, Washington, in 1948. The USS *Pampanito* became in time a museum ship near Fisherman's Wharf in San Francisco; in 1988 the historic fleet there was incorporated into the newly-created San Francisco National Maritime Historic Park.

The year 1988, during which most of this book was written, became a significant year in the lives of the survivors of the *Harrison*. Several events took place which could remind those crewmembers of their days in Shanghai, such as the showing of the film *Empire of the Sun* and the terminal illness of Emperor Hirohito, whom author David Bergamini believed to be the one war criminal who should have been prosecuted but was not. More important, however, were three significant actions of the federal government.

The first of these was the determination that merchant seamen of World War II were entitled to status as veterans of that war. This decision was the culmination of a 10-year administrative and legal process which sought to have merchant seamen included under the provisions of Public Law 95-202.

That law permitted various groups of former civilians in war work to petition the Secretary of Defense who was empowered to grant veterans' status to such people for the purposes of receiving benefits. No rigid criteria for eligibility were established, but the Secretary of Defense--who delegated the authority to the Secretary of the Air Force--was authorized to consider a number of factors in the wartime work of applicant groups. These included the kind of military training received which led to a military capability, the critical nature of missions carried out, the degree of discipline and control including whether individuals could resign, susceptibility to combat assignments, and the perception of individuals that what they were doing equated to active military service.

The first civilians granted veterans' status in 1977 were the former members of the Women's Air Force Service Pilots or WASPs, for whom the legislation had been written. Since that time, 14 other groups had been so recognized, while 50 other groups, including merchant seamen in general, had been denied such status.

Unfortunately, the standards for qualifying seem to have been applied inconsistently and even sentimentally at times. Women's groups have fared well. In addition to the WASPs, the Women's Army Auxiliary Corps (WAACs) and a group of World War I dieticians and therapists had been accepted. Some prisoners had also been recognized, including a group of Navy Department contract employees building Pacific air bases--the Wake Island civilians who were with the *Harrison* officers at Woosung--and a dozen policemen from Guam. Perhaps the strangest ruling was one which authorized veterans' status for about 1,000 merchant seamen who were on ships that were sunk to form a breakwater on the Normandy coast. The subsequent denial of a request by merchant seamen in general led to the final court decision in which a federal judge told the Air Force to implement the granting of veterans' status for the men of the breakwater ships, but also to develop plans and procedures for submission to the court which would open such status to other merchant seamen. On January 20, 1988, the Secretary of the Air Force agreed to accept merchant marine service during the period December 7, 1941, to August 15, 1945, as qualifying for veterans' status.

Some valid opposition had existed to authorizing veterans' status, coming both from military veterans' groups such as the American Legion and from the Defense Department. This opposition centered on the fact that merchant seamen had chosen voluntarily to earn the considerably higher pay and freedom of movement associated with civilian-manned ships over what they would have received in military service. It has generally been assumed that the post-war benefits received only by ex-servicemen, including the GI Bill, compensated veterans for their lack of free choice and their relative low pay during the war.

However, studies done by the Maritime Commission at the end of World War II, and utilized later in connection with the efforts to expand PL 95-202 coverage to include merchant seamen, show that the total monetary compensation for merchant seamen and military personnel during the war had been roughly equal. Granting post-war benefits, such as the GI Bill and VA loans, to military veterans, in effect rewarded them for their loss of personal freedom at the time in their lives when they would otherwise be receiving an education and starting their careers. Granting veterans' status to merchant marine personnel in 1988 would mean that such men would now achieve a residual set of benefits from the Veterans Administration, limited largely to access to VA hospitals and burial benefits.

The Office of the Secretary of the Air Force had backed itself into such an awkward corner by some of the awards it had made that it now made no sense to deny further to merchant seamen in general the veterans' status they had been seeking. Thus, the 1988 decision was made, reversing the earlier position. What would have made more sense a long time ago would have been the granting of veterans' status and benefits to those who experienced the loss of personal freedom similar to that lost by military personnel: all the 5,662 seamen killed and the 600 imprisoned while serving on merchant ships in World War II.

Certain inequities faced by merchant seamen could not be offset by the greater pay and freedom they enjoyed. One was health care benefits, particularly in the case of disabling war-related conditions. Health care for merchant seamen for decades was delivered through the U.S. Public Health Service, and was generally available only to those who were actively sailing--although some care for chronic conditions was offered. With the closing of the Public Health Service hospitals in the 1980s, no health care system remained in place for disabled merchant seamen of those earlier years. Another inequity existed in the foregone opportunities for promotion. While the military services adjusted the rank of ex-prisoners at the end of the war, merchant seamen lost out completely on upgrading their skills and credentials. An ambitious man sailing as an able-bodied seaman or oiler in 1941 could expect to finish the war as a master or chief engineer four years later because of rapid upgrading and promotion opportunities. But if that seaman or oiler spent the war in a prison camp, as did the crew of the *Harrison*, those opportunities were lost forever, and no agency could do anything to help.

Thus, on balance, the inclusion of merchant seamen in the benefits of PL 95-202 may go beyond any obligation the country assumed in 1945 toward its merchant seamen, but it is consistent with the broad interpretation of eligibilty accorded to other applicants under the law, and, more important, it compensates in part for other inequities which have never been addressed.

The second event of 1988 which had significance for the crew of the *Harrison* was the issuance in March of the medal honoring American prisoners of war. Eligibility for this medal came for merchant seamen by virtue of the earlier action by the Secretary of the Air Force granting veterans' status to such seamen.

Authorized by Congress in 1986, the medal features an eagle surrounded by barbed wire and bayonet points. It is inscribed "For Honorable Service While a Prisoner of War." The issuance of the medal to merchant seamen, similar to the granting of veterans' status, is largely symbolic for the recipients; the medal provides tangible recognition to be displayed with other memorabilia of experiences beyond those normally acquired in the merchant service. As noted previously, merchant marine ribbons did exist in World War II. Three area campaign medals and ribbon were issued, along with a victory medal and ribbon and a pre-WW II service ribbon. In addition, a combat ribbon existed, but it was awarded much more sparingly than battle stars were awarded on military campaign ribbons; a ship had to be physically damaged by the enemy to qualify. The higher awards, the Gallant Ship and Distinguished Service Medals, were also awarded on a very restricted basis. Thus, for the crewmembers of the *Harrison* only the Pacific-Middle Eastern campaign ribbon, the pre-war service ribbon and the Victory medal had reflected their brief action at Shaweishan and their long captivity in Shanghai--until the POW medal was issued. It is not clear yet whether the new veterans' status will qualify certain *Harrison* crewmembers posthumously for the Purple Heart: those injured at Shaweishan and those who died there in the ship's screws.

In any case, the POW medal attests to the fact that the crewmembers of the *Harrison* are now recognized formally, albeit belatedly, as real prisoners of war and not as civilian internees. At one point there was some confusion as to whether the *Harrison* crew, representing one quarter of all merchant marine prisoners of World War II, would qualify for the medal since they alone had been treated as civilian internees. But that technicality was overcome, and the crew qualified for the medal, prompting able seaman Howard Allred to observe, "Ironically, I am now listed as a POW."

The final event of 1988 of significance to the crew of the *Harrison* was the granting of reparations by the federal government to the Americans of Japanese descent who were relocated away from coastal California to inland camps in 1942. Little public resentment was expressed at this recent action; in fact, it was generally regarded as an overdue humane gesture for the deprivation accorded these citizens because of their race. But the ex-prisoner community was divided on this issue. While no one denied that the wartime action against the Japanese Americans, in retrospect, seemed harsh, unnecessary and discriminatory, some ex-prisoners and prisoner organizations-- noting how little the federal government had ever done for them--felt that the Japanese government should bear the cost if any reparations were to be made, and that American ex-POWs were equally deserving of such reparations.

For those readers who are offended by this suggestion and feel that such an attitude is vindictive and that there is no excuse for what the federal government did to the relocated Japanese in 1942, these ex-POWs would ask only for an honest re-reading of World War II history. Henry Behrens was told by a Japanese Marine aboard the *Harrison* in Shanghai that his home town of Santa Barbara, California, had been shelled by the Japanese. It was no lie. A Japanese submarine had indeed shelled an oil tank farm at Santa Barbara and producing wells near Ventura; in addition, several tankers were torpedoed within sight of the coast. The West Coast was in near-panic in early 1942. The attack on Pearl Harbor--some small portion of which was aided by Japanese agents in Honolulu--suggested strongly, albeit erroneously in retrospect, that moving Japanese away from the coastal areas of California was necessary for military security. To prisoners returning later from camps with brutal English-speaking guards whose language skills were acquired while living on the West Coast of the United States, the relocation of the American Japanese may not have seemed the injustice that it did to those people born after 1935 who are too young to remember what the first days of the Pacific war were like.

To their credit, most of the ex-prisoners encountered directly or through their recorded statements in the research for this book were not vindictive, and had no problems with the reparations for the relocated Japanese Americans. Most, however, would have agreed with Dr. William Foley, who survived the Oriental water torture at the hands of an ex-Honolulu taxi driver. Foley observed, "I would have preferred that in enacting this legislation Congress would have added to the bill a sense-of-Congress statement to the effect that the Japanese Empire had inflicted grievous harm on a number of prisoners of war held in its prison camps during World War II."

With these significant events of 1988 noted, the final elements of this strange tale may now be logged. The story of Voyage 55 of the SS *President Harrison* has taken far longer to conclude than anyone associated with the ship might have expected. Perhaps it still may not be over; some treasure seeker might yet decide to raise the ship from her resting place 360 feet below the surface of the South China Sea--in search of the bones of Peking Man. But, much more likely, the last remaining bit of the story to be completed will probably be the unheralded passing of the final survivor of the crew.

What did it all mean, this confusing series of events surrounding the enemy's capture and use of a large American passenger liner? And what are the lessons of military and maritime history to be gleaned from the unusual story? In the final chapter of this book we will reflect on what it all seems to have counted for in terms of the judgments of history. But, first, we need to dispose of one fascinating loose end--the fate of Peking Man.

Chapter 11

Peking Man

The most intriguing sub-plot to emerge from the story of the *President Harrison* is that involving the disappearance of the bones of Peking Man. Concurrent with the capture of the Marines in North China who had been entrusted with the responsibility for safeguarding these priceless remains, and the capture of the *President Harrison* which was scheduled to evacuate those Marines, came the disappearance of the famous fossils.

After the war was over and it became clear that the bones had never turned up anywhere, the full impact of the loss of the fossils hit the scientific community. Henry L. Shapiro of the American Museum of Natural History, in his book *Peking Man*, assessed the loss: "Never in the history of the recovery of the fossil record of human evolution had there been a disaster of such magnitude, for these ancient bones represented a veritable population of at least 40 individuals--men, women, and children-- from a stage of human evolution previously unknown."

Curiosity about the fate of Peking Man was not confined to the scholarly world. With the lifting of the "Bamboo Curtain" after President Richard Nixon's historic trip to China in 1972 the Peking Man story became a subject of considerable interest to the general public during the 1970s. This interest was enhanced by a series of magazine articles and books which had been generated by the interaction of several key people: Dr. William T. Foley, the ex-Navy physician from North China who was then casting about for information to include in his memoirs; Dr. Shapiro, who had learned for the first time of Dr. Foley's reported connections with the bones; and Christopher Janus, a midwestern stock broker who had inveigled a hard-to-get visa to visit China, where he unexpectedly was commissioned by the communist government to find the missing anthropological treasure. After Foley published an article on Peking Man in the Cornell University Medical College *Alumnus Quarterly* in late 1971, Shapiro and Janus each produced books on the subject in 1974 and 1975 respectively. In all these sources the extensive involvement of the North China Marines as the final custodians of Peking Man was described, along with possible explanations of the disappearance of the bones.

Speculation on the fate of Peking Man centered on a cluster of theories. These included (a) the bones were discarded as trash by Japanese soldiers who had no idea of their value, perhaps to be eaten later by Chinese peasants as medicinal "dragon teeth;" (b) the remains were stolen by such diverse suspects as American Marines or Chinese war lords; (c) the bones were removed to safety by responsible museum officials, possibly from Taiwan or even Japan; or (4) the fossils were lost in being loaded aboard the *Harrison* or in the subsequent grounding of the vessel.

This last theory reflects the fact that post-war scientific researchers knew only of the scheduled role of the ship in removing the bones, not her actual fate. The long-time curator of the bones in Peking, Dr. Franz Weidenreich, died in America in 1948, apparently still believing that the bones had been lost while being loaded aboard the ship. As late as 1959 the authoritative journal *Science* editorialized that it was unfortunate that no further search for the bones had been made after the *Harrison* ran aground with the Marines and three cases of the bones on board on December 8, 1941, near Shanghai.

Even though an American President Lines investigation in 1972 and the books and articles on the subject of Peking Man in the mid-1970s made it clear that the *Harrison* never came any closer to Chinwangtao than 700 miles, a shadow of doubt continues to remain over the ship. As Christopher Janus observed in his ghost-written book, "Though hardly a mystery ship laden with treasure, the *Harrison* was never completely absolved of its connection with Peking Man." It is for this reason that the following material has been included in this account of the *Harrison*'s adventures on the China coast, even though the story may seem a bit extraneous to military history or ship buffs. In fact, if may seem more like a detective story than World War II history.

Most explanations of the fate of Peking Man have concentrated on events following the departure of the bones from Peking, and consequently assume that the initial disappearance occurred along the projected route to Chinwangtao and to the

President Harrison. However, the evidence concerning how the bones were handled prior to leaving Peking is so contradictory as to suggest that any subesquent shipment of the bones should be regarded as a possibility, rather than as a fact.

As noted in an earlier chapter, the story of the removal of the bones from Peking is full of inexplicable discrepancies from the very beginning. The three accounts mentioned earlier are the source of most of the reported details concerning the movement of the bones. The books by Shapiro and Janus were based on interviews with people involved in the original shipment, while the article by Dr. Foley was based on his first-hand recollections of events in North China during the war years. Unfortunately, in each of these accounts, the original source of certain key information is not provided.

A fourth major source of information departs significantly from the others in having an Asian, rather than an American perspective. Consisting of a series of articles on the disappearance of Peking Man which appeared in 1980 in *Yomiuri Shinbun*, a leading Tokyo newspaper, this source is often at odds with the others.

For example, on such a basic question as who packed the bones there are surprisingly different points of view. It is generally agreed that the officials of the U.S.-sponsored Peking Union Medical College wanted the remains of Peking Man shipped out of China for safekeeping, and that the packing of the bones was initially assigned to Claire Taschdjian who had been Dr. Weidenreich's assistant before his return to the States earlier that year. Janus indicates that she had been provided an assistant on this project, unnamed and otherwise unidentified in this account. However, Ms. Taschdjian in later years claimed to have done all the work herself. The 1980 series in the *Yomiuri Shinbun*, written by Takashi Toda, contains an interview with a Chinese man named Hu Chen Zhi, a technician at the Chinese Geological Museum; he claimed to have been ordered by Ms. Taschdjian to pack the boxes, a responsibility he carried out with the help of an engineer from the "dissection lab" at the medical school. This work was completed in two hours time, according to this man, rather than the three days that Janus claims Ms. Taschdjian spent on the project.

Thus, it is difficult to know whom to believe. But the question of who packed the boxes may be relatively unimportant

153

in the total series of events. At least at this point it has been clearly established that the bones were packed at the college, making this episode the last one in which the Peking Man story can actually be verified.

The contradictions continue, however. Perhaps the most fundamental one in the various accounts concerns the question of *how* the bones were packed, inasmuch as this detail affected how they could be handled during shipment or storage. Using Ms. Taschdjian as his source, Janus described the original boxes into which the bones were placed as cardboard, and indicated that they were then put into two redwood crates, one marked **A** and the other marked **B**. Ms. Taschdjian later characterized these wooden boxes as about the size of military footlockers, although not as high. They were fitted with metal locks and hinges.

Another discrepancy, relatively insignificant but nevertheless puzzling, developed over whether any glass jars were used in packing some of the small bones. Ms. Taschdjian has insisted that no glass was used, but the technician who claimed to have packed the bones said that such jars were used in packing teeth. Shapiro, who felt that glass was an inappropriate container for anthropological specimens, was confused by Dr. Foley's claim to have also seen the bones packed in glass jars since Foley was not present at the packing.

Still another account of the last days of the Marines in North China, which deals only briefly with Peking Man, provides further contradictory evidence about the packing of the bones. Colonel John A. White who (as a captain) was executive officer at Tientsin in 1941, writing in the *United States Marines in North China*, reports what Colonel Ashurst said as he shared his knowledge of the packing and shipping of the remains with some of his officers. "I had my name stencilled on the several otherwise unmarked fresh pine boxes with dimensions of about 1 by 2 by 4 feet," said Colonel Ashurst, according to White. Presumably, an observer would be able to tell the difference between white pine and the redwood mentioned in the Janus account, as well as the difference between an unmarked box and one marked with an **A** or **B**.

Additional support for the notion of a white pine box over the redwood box comes from Shapiro who reported what he learned in correspondence with Dr. Pei Wen-Chung, a Chinese

The principal locations of the Peking Man story in North China are shown on this map.

A key figure in the Peking Man story is Dr. William T. Foley, shown here en route home after the war. (William T. Foley, M.D.)

Colonel Ashurst had much on his mind in late 1941, so Peking Man did not receive as much attention from him as anthropologists might have wished. (John A. White)

Camp Holcomb at Chinwangtao looked more like a peaceful village that the military post where the bones of Peking Man may have disappeared. (U.S. Marine Corps)

This reconstruction shows how Peking Man may have looked according to anthropologists. (American Museum of Natural History)

The notorious footlocker belonging to the widow of the Marine actually had some promising bones in it. (American Museum of Natural History)

geologist who had discovered the first skull of *Sinanthropus Pekinensis*. Pei claimed to have assisted in the packing of the remains in "two white wooden boxes," although he had reported earlier that he had no role in the packing process. Hu Chen Zhi, the man who claimed to have packed the boxes, described them as being made of white pine wood, of footlocker proportions, with the designation *Case 1* "inscribed" on the larger box and *Case 2* on the slightly smaller second box.

To continue the Janus/Taschdjian account, the wooden boxes were padlocked, and put into the college vault. A week later two padlock keys were presented to Ms. Taschdjian by a Marine officer who remarked that the mission had been accomplished, presumably meaning that the Marines now had the remains safely in their possession. However, Trevor Bowen, the college administrator, testified later to an investigator that he delivered *three* boxes to Colonel Ashurst at the Marine barracks. Partial confirmation of this action comes from a letter written to Shapiro by Mary E. Ferguson, the medical college registrar at the time, but her explanation may raise as many questions as it answers. She wrote, "From my office window I watched Mr. Bowen taking a locker trunk across the marble court to the front gate of the College to a car in which it went to the U.S. Marine barracks. Whether or not there was more than one locker trunk, I cannot say, but I can vouch for there having been at least one."

There are several problems in this explanation. Ms. Ferguson acknowledged that there may have been more than one "locker trunk," so there may not be any contradiction of Bowen in the number of items he moved. But it is her description of the item in question as a "locker trunk," rather than boxes as reported by Bowen, that raises a question: Would a wooden box with metal hinges and hasp be perceived as a "locker trunk"? There may also have been a unjustified presumption on Mrs. Ferguson's part that the otherwise unidentified car was going to the Marine barracks.

In a key passage with no attribution as to source, Janus asserts that Colonel Ashurst "ordered the collection transferred from the redwood crates to regular Marine footlockers." Colonel Ashurst's report to the Marine Corps does not mention this transfer; nor does Foley's article. Presumably this transfer took place after the Marines took possession of the bones, but if

Ms. Ferguson saw footlockers rather than boxes, perhaps a transfer had already been made in the college vault. How and by whom this transfer was accomplished--if indeed it happened--remains the most critical question in the post-Peking phase of the disappearance of the bones, yet no writer has shown any curiosity about the lack of corroboration of this alleged transfer.

Shapiro is ready to acknowledge that,

> *Certain events seem clearly established. There can be little doubt that the fossils were, in fact, packed and prepared for shipment to the United States by the Chinese and American officials of the Peking Union Medical College and the Cenezoic Research Laboratory. The records and witnesses for this are abundant and clear. It is also well authenticated that at least two boxes containing these relics were delivered to the Marine Corps in Peking for transferral by train to Camp Holcomb in Tientsin [sic], where they were to await the S.S.* **President Harrison** *for shipment to the United States. That these bones reached Camp Holcomb is also confirmed by reliable sources.*

Perhaps. But there is no clear eye-witness evidence that established that the fossils were ever again known to be in a given box or footlocker after they were deposited in the college vault. Expressing the problem semantically, to have a disappearance one must earlier have had an appearance; the bones had never appeared to any American, Marine or civilian, during or after their packing.

Obviously, the U.S. Marine Corps and the college shared jointly in the secret of when and how the relics were moved; possibly the embassy was also involved. In the absence of the ambassador, Nelson T. Johnson, who had relocated to Chungking, the embassy staff originally had declined to permit the use of diplomatic pouches to bring out the bones; now they would certainly be expected to have some knowledge of the alternative method which had been selected. Subsequently, according to Shapiro, the ambassador by telegram in mid-November authorized the shipment of the bones.

Through the years the Marines may not have told their side of the story as completely as they could have. Immediately after the war an official inquiry was conducted by the Marine Corps, but the investigator in Peking, Lieutenant Albert Scalcione, was unable to develop any reliable information which would throw any new light on the mystery. Other investigators in Tientsin and Chinwangtao drew similar blanks in their search for traces of the fossils. A file has been maintained on the case through the years, but the Corps has no official position on the involvement of any of its personnel.

There was, of course, considerably more to the story of the disappearance of the bones of Peking Man than merely how the bones were packed. In fact, most later accounts of the disappearance devote much more attention to later events than to the packing. The attention devoted in this chapter to the packing of the bones, which may seem excessive to the reader, and the parallel neglect of other more colorful aspects of the story simply highlight the uncertainty which characterized this entire sequence of events from the very outset. Without some assurance that the bones were in the containers in which they were assumed to be, everything that followed has to be regarded as speculation, not fact, making any theory of the disappearance of the bones as valid as the next.

These subsequent events were interesting and exciting. Various accounts have focused considerable attention on:

● the train guarded by Marines that supposedly took the lockers to Chinwangtao, and whether the relics actually arrived at Camp Holcomb or were captured enroute by the Japanese;

● the presence of the bones in some of Dr. Foley's footlockers on which Pharmacist Mate Herman Davis mounted a machine-gun for the short-lived defense of that facility;

● the possibility that the bones may have been taken from the captured footlockers before the baggage was later returned to Dr. Foley at Tientsin, after which he inexplicably never opened the trunks;

● whether the bones may have been in personal baggage that Dr. Foley left at various locations in Tientsin;

● whether the bones may have been in footlockers carried by the Marines from prison camp to prison camp throughout most of the war, only to be lost as the prisoners were sent to Japan toward the end of the war;

● or how the footlockers were uniquely vulnerable to theft or pilferage at so many times and places.

In his book Janus describes the major thrusts of his search during the 1970s to locate the bones of Peking Man. Each of these efforts suggest a different theory of what happened to the bones. Singled out for extensive treatment by Janus are the following aspects of his search, some which have all the elements of a cloak-and-dagger novel.

The first important activity was his contact with a secretive woman who claimed to be the widow of a Marine who had stolen the bones. After meeting Janus at a rendezvous atop the Empire State Building in New York City this woman sent the researcher a picture of the bones, which some anthropologists, using comparisons with plaster casts of the bones brought out of China by Dr. Weidenreich earlier in 1941, later considered to be authentic. The woman then dropped from sight, to be replaced by her "attorney"--a man who seemed interested only in what the bones were worth in the market place.

Janus next describes his contact with a Chinese-American businessman named Andrew Sze of New York City who insisted that a friend of his in Taiwan had the bones. Sze strongly criticized Janus for being unaware of the grave danger involved in openly seeking information about the present location of Peking Man, danger which was generated in part by his widely-circulated offer of a reward. Janus subsequently went to Taiwan to check out the Sze story, then on to Hong Kong and southeast Asia. At each stop, the designated custodian of the bones had said, "No, I don't have them, but I know who does."

Finally, Janus evidences a growing suspicion that the man who holds the key to the fate of Peking Man is the prominent New York City cardiologist, Dr. William T. Foley, in whose footlockers many years ago the bones once reposed--at least according to the commonly held theory. To Janus, Foley has been less than forthright in declining to discuss the case fully in order to protect certain unnamed friends in China with whom he left some of his belongings in 1941. Janus summed up Foley this way: "He was a man with a thirty-year history of dealings with the Chinese and Japanese, in some of the most brutal circumstances imaginable, and he seemed to have acquired a measure of the fabled inscrutability of the Orient."

Only one new lead of any significance has surfaced since Janus published his book in 1975. The *New York Times* reported in 1980 that Janus was planning to go to Peking to check out a story told by an ex-Marine, Roger Ames, from a hospital bed in Dallas. Ames claimed that he had been on guard duty at the gate of the legation in Peking late in the evening on December 7, 1941, when two Marine officers carried a footlocker outside the gate and buried it close by. The chances of finding such a spot may be slim; the American ambassador in Peking told Janus that the United States no longer owns the old legation property, and that something else may have been built on it by now.

Another ex-Marine, R. J. Innes, told Janus that a footlocker with the bones in it had been in the captain's cabin on the *Awa Maru* when that vessel, although guaranteed safe passage by the Allies, had been sunk by the submarine *Queenfish* in 1945 in the Formosa Straits. Innes did not disclose how he could claim this knowledge. A Chinese salvage crew raised part of this ship in 1978, but found none of the treasure of gold and diamonds the ship reportedly had carried--and no bones of Peking Man.

None of these avenues of exploration has led Christopher Janus anywhere. Even with the help of the FBI, made possible because of the friendly overtures to mainland China being made at the time by President Richard Nixon and Secretary of State Henry Kissinger, Janus could not locate the Marine widow or anyone else with real knowledge of the case. No part of the $250,000 reward Janus offered for information leading to the return of the bones of Peking Man has apparently ever been paid.

For the record, Dr. Foley has recently indicated that there is "a 25 per cent chance" that the bones may yet be among some of his belongings in China. But he is still reluctant to visit the country to facilitate the search, insisting that what he has already said has made life difficult for his friends there, and that he might be grilled extensively and perhaps even detained if he were to return to the country he once knew so well. Foley is realistic, a trait that annoyed Janus. In keeping with that realism, he still repeats the line attributed to him by Janus, "Nobody throws anything away in China," but he says it today with a wry smile on his face.

Perhaps the money offered by Janus as a reward might be better spent as a prize in a contest for the most interesting yet plausible explanation of how the bones of Peking Man disappeared. Obviously, the dramatic elements of the mystery are worth developing. In 1977 Claire Taschdjian wrote a novel called *The Peking Man Is Missing*. The reviewer in the *New York Times*, after praising the author's knowledge of fossil anatomy, disposed of the book by saying that "suspense writing involves just as many skills as paleoanatomy, but they are not, it seems, the same skills."

Films were a natural medium for the story. The dust jacket of the Janus book announced, "Soon To Be a Major Motion Picture." That film, however, was never made, but a television version of the story was. Some years ago an episode of the television series "Hawaii Five-O" centered on a Marine footlocker suspected of containing the bones, which upon arrival in Honolulu turned out to contain instead the body of a murdered Marine. An even wilder tale of murder and intrigue among evil men contending for the bones has been scripted by an English film production outfit, but fortunately they seem to have run out of money with which to produce their gory story. On a less fictional level, during the time when interest in Peking Man was high, the Canadian Broadcasting Corporation produced a television documentary which included a number of interviews with key figures in the story.

One element of the post war research on the disappearance of Peking Man has even become a story itself. In February 1981, Christopher Janus was indicted by a grand jury in a federal district court in Chicago on 37 counts of fraud growing out of his raising of $640,000 for further development of the Peking Man story, including the film. Of this amount, $520,000 came from bank loans and $120,000 from private investors. Charged with diverting the funds to his own use, Janus pled guilty to two counts of the indictment; the other 35 were dropped by the federal government. Earlier involvement with the bones of Peking Man had led to captivity for the North China Marines and the crew of the *Harrison*; whether this final involvement with those bones by Christopher Janus led to his captivity has not been determined at this point.

Related to the disappearance of the fossils are several appealing possibilities that have been suggested but not actually explored by researchers. Three are close enough to the mainstream of this book to merit further review.

One is that the two Marine officers who went "duck hunting" from Camp Holcomb on December 8, 1941, actually may have somehow disposed of the bones while they were away from the camp. Janus quotes one North China Marine, the man who had awakened Lieutenant Huizenga and Warrant Officer Lee to go on this trip, as having doubts about what the two men really did while they were away. That man died during the writing of this book, before he could be interviewed.

There are indeed questions to be raised concerning this story. On a Monday morning with a number of things yet to be done to get ready for the arrival of the *Harrison* within 48 hours, and with a military alert in effect which anticipated hostilities within a few days, why would the two highest-ranking men in the unit decide to go duck hunting, particularly on a morning with temperatures of 40 degrees below zero? Why, too, would they take a truck, rather than a staff car? Why do official Marine Corps histories report that Huizenga was "supervising the stockpiling of supplies for the expected arrival of the *President Harrison*" in the pre-dawn hours of that morning while the eyewitness accounts have him off on a duck hunting trip?

An equally intriguing theory concerns the *President Harrison* in a more direct way. As the ship loaded the 4th Marines in Shanghai in late November a steel safe was brought aboard under heavy guard. That safe was guarded by a sentry, night and day, and went ashore, still under guard, when the ship reached the Philippines. The contents may have been known to the Marines, but Captain Pierson was never told what was in the safe. While the safe may well have contained important records, cash, or even bullion being taken out of China for safe keeping, it might also have contained the bones of Peking Man.

What was to prevent officials in Peking from creating an elaborate diversion by apparently shipping the bones to Chinwangtao, but actually sending them quietly on an earlier occasion to Shanghai? Although he does not mention this theory, the thought must have occurred to Janus who quotes

Lieutenant George Newton, the Marine officer who made the final courier trip from Peking to Shanghai, as saying that no such material was carried on that trip. Newton asserted that "The shipment was not made through that port or on the *President Harrison*." But how could he know that?

Newton later acknowledged that as a Marine junior officer he was not privy to any real information about the movement of the bones of Peking Man. His courier trip to Shanghai was by a British coastal steamer, not by rail, so he was in no position to say that a shipment had not been made.

Still another explanation of what happened to the bones supports the Shanghai connection. John Carey, an APL employee in Shanghai in 1941, remembers being told by the company agent Henry Kay to be particularly careful with certain Marine baggage he was loading on the *President Madison* because the boxes in question were very important. Carey later concluded that at that moment he must have participated in the loading of the bones of Peking Man aboard the ship. His reasoning adds a new dimension to Peking Man theories, one involving the Jesuit order. He recalls seeing two passengers watching from the deck above with great interest as the boxes in question were stowed into the hold of the *Madison*; these men were priests. Carey later learned that one of the most prominent experts on *Sinanthropus Pekinensis* who remained in China during the war was the Jesuit priest Pierre Teilhard de Chardin, a man with whom Dr. William T. Foley once studied philosophy. Carey felt that this Jesuit connection could easily explain how the bones left China for the safety of the United States. It is interesting to note, however, that Captain Valedmar Nielsen of the *Madison* has no recollection or knowledge of such a shipment.

Exact dates are curiously missing from most accounts of the packing of the bones, and their acceptance by the Marine Corps. An exception is the Japanese newspaper series which offers two sets of dates, one involving the two Chinese who allegedly packed the bones--which would have allowed enough time to send the bones to Shanghai--and the other more conventional timetable covering their shipment to Chinwangtao.

With something as irreplaceable and valuable as these bones were, it also seems odd that they were apparently not receipted for in some fashion at each stage of their transmittal. If the absence of this prudent practice was attributable to the need for secrecy, one can only conclude that secrecy prevailed, but the bones did not. But if the absence of checks on the location of the bones reflected a lack of time or a general deterioration of standard military procedures under the exigencies of war, then it seems even less likely that duck hunting would be a rational or permissible activity under this state of near-siege. Thus, there are inexplicable inconsistencies in accounts of Marine behavior at Chinwangtao.

Of course, in both of these interesting and speculative scenarios no measurable outcome was attained. If Huizenga and Lee did stash the bones somewhere, then all the conjecture about what went on in Chinwangtao *after* the capture comes back into play--the "tumultuous tragedy of Camp Holcomb" as it was described by the physical anthropologist Carleton S. Coon. And, if the bones were carried out of China on the *Harrison* to the Philippines, then the rapid collapse of the military and political situation there would have required the creation of still another scheme to get the bones to safety in the States.

But what if the bones were on the *Madison*? They would not have to be taken off in the Philippines, because the ship had cargo for Singapore and beyond. She eventually reached New York. What an interesting possibility this scenario represents!

In the absence of any evidence that either of those basic scenarios was ever played out, or that any alternative theory of the disappearance of the bones has any more validity than any other, it is difficult to form any meaningful conclusion as to any possible connection between the *President Harrison* and Peking Man. Perhaps one might hesitatingly infer that if the bones were actually shipped from Peking to Chinwangtao, then the *Harrison* could not have been involved in their further movement. But if the bones did not go to Chinwangtao, then conceivably the *Harrison*--or even the *Madison*--might have been involved in their disappearance. In the latter case, the responsible ship would then belong to a select group of people and institutions with links to the loss of the famous fossils, links that are at the same time both tortuous and tenuous.

Better planning by the staff of the Commander, Asiatic Fleet, might have spared the *Harrison* and the Marines from captivity, and the bones of Peking Man from oblivion. (Steamship Historical Society of America)

Chapter 12

Judgments of History

It would be relatively easy, and even tempting, to conclude in the case of the *President Harrison* that, all things considered, everything turned out all right. After all, the North China Marines fared far better by being stranded in China than if they had been evacuated to the Philippines; the fate of the 4th Marines was not affected by the capture of the ship; and the crew of the *Harrison* traded away, albeit involuntarily, the risk of further participation in the war at sea for the relative security of captivity with deprivation. One might even argue that, while 16 men were lost, most of whom were at least middle aged, that number was not much different than one would expect for the normal death rate for a crew of that age over a 45-month period when superimposed on the general wartime death rate for merchant seamen.

This reasoning might be accepted by some with Pollyannish tendencies, those who say "things have a way of turning out for the best"; or by those with a pragmatic "muddle through" perspective of history who believe that "any landing you can walk away from is a good landing"; or by those, including several *Harrison* crewmembers who offered their counsel during the writing of this book, who say, "let bygones be bygones." Indeed, most of us must live our personal lives in this passive way, settling uncritically for the best that we can get from life under the circumstances that have been dealt to us by fate, and accepting that fate stoically.

As an explanation of the events of history, however, that approach is inappropriate. It represents a gutless capitulation to a convenient determinism that ignores the hard questions of causation and responsibility, or even of right and wrong. Governments and governmental officials need to be held accountable for their actions, earning praise if the results are beneficial and censure if the results lead to deprivation and death for the affected citizens. In the case of the *President Harrison* it is true that the outcome might have been far worse than it was, but it is equally true that the loss of 16 lives, the detainment and imprisonment of more than 150 people for three years and nine months, and the surrender to the enemy of a valuable transport--which may have moved as many as 20,000 troops during her service for the Japanese--might conceivably have been prevented entirely. Thus, an honest and critical assessment ought to be made, to assign responsibility for what happened, good and bad, and to learn any historical lessons that may be derived from the events surrounding the loss of the ship.

The decisions that affected the *President Harrison* and her crew were of three broad types. First were a series of geopolitical or strategic decisions regarding the American positions in the Far East made by the President, the State Department and high-level military planners. Second were the tactical decisions made prior to and during the war by military commanders in the Pacific, together with those decisions made for logistic reasons by these military commanders. The final group of decisions was of a legal nature, made by the courts and the Congress after the war.

It is difficult to discuss the first set of decisions without getting caught up in the whole question of responsibility for Pearl Harbor and America's lack of preparedness for the Pacific war. However, rather than become unduly involved in an analysis of such factors as the agreements between Roosevelt and Churchill concerning the priorities of global war, the most practical and generous way to proceed may be simply to start from the premise that the United States had underestimated Japan.

Obviously, the Rainbow War Plan was unrealistic, in that it assumed that the Pacific Fleet could battle its way across the Pacific within six months and provide the necessary support for American forces that were fighting for time against the Japanese. One side of the equation almost worked in that Corregidor held out for five months, but there was no fleet--nor even resupply convoys--to provide the means for surviving and ultimately for winning. In the plaintive song of the "Battling Bastards of Bataan," there was indeed "no momma, no poppa, no Uncle Sam." Americans in the Far East had been let down by their government. While Pearl Harbor had knocked out major elements of the Pacific Fleet, there should have been enough sealift capability of transports and escorts to bring a major expeditionary force across the Pacific. But the capability did not exist, and the force was needed elsewhere.

The indecision of the State Department over the American posture and presence in the Far East also contributed to the low state of readiness there. Realistically the Department had ordered American dependents home a year before the war began, but it had kept the small Marine detachments in China to show the flag. While Roosevelt's decision to order the embargo on oil shipments to Japan was necessary, that decision marked the end of any pretext of business as usual in the Orient. The Marines became sacrificial lambs on the altar of a vanishing world of extraterritoriality. The Shanghai Marines were fortunate that, in the face of unrealistic thinking and haphazard planning, they could still be evacuated, but they were unfortunate, of course, in that the American strongholds in the Philippines to which they withdrew proved to be anything but strongholds. The North China Marines were forsaken, too, in that the diplomatic efforts to gain their repatriation were abandoned early in order not to jeopardize the chances of repatriation for other Americans in the Orient. A vigorous planned diplomatic effort in behalf of the Marines might have spared the *Harrison* her fateful voyage.

Thus, from a geopolitical or grand strategy perspective the fate of the *President Harrison*, as well as that of the military forces she was impressed into service to transport was preordained under the policies and priorities of the American war effort. Failure and fallback, slaughter and surrender, defeat and degradation--these alliterative spectors were the lot of the Asiatic Fleet and American ground and air forces in the Far East in 1941 and 1942.

Regional military commanders were powerless to change any of the broad political and military policies emanating from Washington. But they did have power to make tactical decisions affecting how these policies were implemented in specific situations. In the case of the *Harrison* her assignment to the Chinwangtao mission more than three weeks after Admiral Hart received the green light to bring out the Marines seems ill-timed and ill-advised. Why could the Navy not have requisitioned a ship immediately to make the trip? Why was it not possible to bring the two groups of Marines out of China simultaneously? Why was it not possible to provide a submarine escort for the *Harrison*, an escort that might have disposed of the troublesome *Nagasaki Maru*? Later in the war why could military intelligence not have known about 2,000 Allied troops embarked in two transports leaving the former British bastion of Singapore?

Even though its muddled staff planning prior to the outbreak of the war cannot be excused, the collapse of the Asiatic Fleet can be understood in the face of the enormous odds that it faced with such miniscule resources. It is somewhat harder to accept the reality that, later in the war when American naval strength was at its peak, the Navy knew so little of the whereabouts and status of the *Harrison*.

Obviously, as a Japanese ship the *Harrison* did not merit any special effort on the part of naval intelligence beyond that given to all other Japanese merchant ships. But she somehow came to symbolize the hell ships and the thousands of Allied prisoners who died by American hands while being transported aboard them. If we were unable to know anything of our own ship within this fleet, how could we expect to know anything about the rest of these ships?

Quite possibly the tactical problems encountered or created by the planners of the Asiatic Fleet were largely logistics problems. These problems included unrealistic thinking about moving the two groups of Marines out of China. In both cases, even though the warning accurately predicting the start of the war had been received by the Asiatic Fleet, the withdrawal was treated as a peacetime permanent change of station rather than as a wartime retreat to rescue men from the danger of captivity. Both the units and the men were allowed to bring out everything they had, representing hundreds of tons of cargo for the ships. In the end, most of the personal belongings were lost, with the 4th Marines torching theirs at a warehouse at Olongapo when they withdrew from that area, and the North China Marines losing their ubiquitous footlockers--including, perhaps, those containing the bones of Peking Man--at Chinwangtao and at various camps along the route to Japan.

If the North China Marines had been made to travel light and had been dispatched by rail to Shanghai to join the 4th Marines leaving on the *Harrison* and the *Madison*, all the Marines could have left China together, and the *Harrison*, like the *Madison*, could have gone home. Thus, that legendary Marine Corps duty in China, with its insidious influence on personnel to acquire all kinds of worldly goods and souvenirs, had burdened down the men of the 4th Regiment and the North China Marines, and no one on the staff of the Asiatic Fleet saw how this heavy burden of baggage would interfere in the evacuation of these troops.

Another logistics problems, created by officials of American President Lines rather than by the Navy, was sending the *Harrison* north from Manila with only enough fuel for the round trip to Chinwangtao, plus 10 percent. This action precluded any possibility of escape for the ship, if she had been able to shake off the *Nagasaki Maru* and make it through the Ryukyu chain to the open Pacific Ocean. The company, too, might have offered the passenger-oriented members of the steward's department the opportunity to stay in Manila while the ship was making the Chinwangtao trip, although as it turned out, civilians including seamen at large in Manila were to get very little chance to be evacuated later.

The final set of decisions affecting the outcome of the war on the crew of the *Harrison* was made after the fact. The court cases, which initially went against the seamen and required an appeal to a higher court to overturn, showed the insensitivity of the federal government, as owner of APL and as a third-party intercessor, to what the crew had been forced to endure as a result of having tried to carry out a military objective of the government in 1941. The War Claims Act, with its initial disregard of merchant seamen, was further evidence that remarkably little thought had been given in governmental circles to the 600 mariners who had been captured by the enemy through no fault or decision on their part.

True, the events of 1988 have belatedly, albeit grudgingly, moved to correct the attitude of neglect and disinterest which had prevailed on the part of the federal government toward merchant seamen of World War II, particularly those who had been prisoners. But it took more than 40 years, plus some glaringly inconsistent decisions by the Secretary of the Air Force which he could not justify without granting veterans' status to merchant seamen, before this corrective action was finally taken. Thus, by outliving the opposition and by default, merchant seamen have finally prevailed over the federal bureaucracy.

History, then, is likely to find fault with the President and the State Department for creating the geopolitical and strategic climate in which the *Harrison* was forced to sail to Chinwangtao; the staff of the Asiatic Fleet and the American President Lines for the tactical/logistics decision making that set the rules for that trip; the intelligence establishment for not knowing more about the Japanese ships carrying Allied prisoners; and the courts and Congress for their reluctance and slowness in rectifying the wrongs done to captured merchant seamen.

There are positive dimensions to the judgments of history, however. The *Harrison* story points up one significant success story: the role of the World War I Shipping Board transports in supplying much-needed trooplift capacity early in World War II when newer ships were not available in sufficient numbers. All three classes of these ships justified their construction as dual purpose ships: passenger liners and transports. The seven 502s all became transports or hospital ships; in addition to the *Harrison*, two were lost, the *President Taylor* at Canton Island and the *President Grant* at New Guinea. The 12 535s remaining under the American flag at the start of the war also served as transports; two of these ships were also lost, both in North African landings as Navy troop ships, the *Hugh L. Scott*, ex-*President Pierce*, and the *Tasker H. Bliss*, ex-*President Cleveland*. Even the Hog Islanders saw considerable war service: the five that had always been Army or Navy vessels served throughout the war, although all but one of the others--which had all been peacetime Army transports at one time--were casualties of the war as Belgian ships. Thus, the Shipping Board construction program of World War I paid big dividends in World War II.

Perhaps not as successful was the concept of Naval Reserve ships, a concept which had existed in law for a number of years but had never really been tested. The *Harrison*'s conscription in Manila in 1941 was an opportunity to test the concept from an operational perspective. There was no time to convert the ship fully to a troop ship, and to provide the armament and other equipment that most of American transports were soon to acquire. But there seemed to be no reservoir of ideas within the headquarters of the Asiatic Fleet with which to effect a quick call-up of a Naval Reserve ship. Other than erecting some wooden bunks in the holds and latrines or benjos at the deck edges, no other actions were taken to convert quickly a passenger ship into a funtional troop ship. At a minimum, with the ship facing possible encounters with the enemy, the Navy might have provided an armed guard with mobile weapons, demolition charges for scuttling, additional fuel oil, and some alternative escape plans, together with external support such as escorts. In other words, while the *Harrison* was sufficiently prepared for the mission, the military planners were not.

170

Up to this point considerable blame and a limited amount of praise has been assigned to individuals, organizations, and concepts which affected the outcome of the *President Harrison* affair. In closing out the analysis of this unusual series of events it is time to consider once again the people of the ship, and the role they played in minimizing the impact of their own capture and the loss of the ship.

Although there were other ships whose crews were imprisoned after the vessels were lost, the *President Harrison* was unique in that she, along with the *Admiral Y. S. Williams*, was one of only two merchant ships to be captured. Thus, the noteworthiness of her capture was in its singularity, not its significance or value as a military triumph. She was the first ship to be captured, the largest ship to be captured, the ship whose crew spent longer in captivity than any other, the only passenger ship to be captured, and the only ship to be scuttled by stranding--but all these comparisions made her first among two. Thus, it is apparent that her capture at the "battle of Shaweishan Island" counted for relatively little as a military accomplishment in the history of the war in the Pacific.

And yet, by depriving the Japanese of the use of the ship for at least four months and possibly even longer, Captain Pierson and his crew were able to effect a real, albeit unmeasurable, delay in Japan's ability to deliver troops and cargo somewhere in the Far East. The punitive treatment that the captain received at the hands of his captors was an obvious expression of their displeasure over the temporary loss of the ship. After the war Captain Pierson learned from friends in Kobe just how close he had come to being executed for the stranding of the ship.

The captain and crew handled their captivity with considerable equanimity and common sense. Quite possibly, other American merchant seamen would have done as well; certainly those from the *Vincent* and *Malama* behaved in much the same way as did the *Harrison* officers with whom they shared life in the prison camps. But it was the *Harrison*'s crew that was called upon to test its mettle. This crew was more than a typical ship's crew; because of its large steward's department not found on freighters, it was much more of a melting pot of nationalities, ages and conditions of health than one would expect to find on a smaller ship. The 13 who died in Shanghai epitomized the marginal side of the mix; the vast majority of the crew who survived personified the resilience and resourcefulness of

American merchant seamen.

If it had to happen, this confrontation between Japanese naval forces and an American passenger ship, there could have been no better-equipped group of Americans to prevail over the resultant adversity than the men and one woman who were aboard the *President Harrison* at Shaweishan. It is unlikely that they will ever be singled out as heroes of World War II, but they ought to be remembered as outstanding examples of a proud and colorful breed of American merchant seamen who did what was asked of them, and more. Both the *Harrison*'s crew and the larger total of 250,000 merchant seamen made contributions in World War II which have long been overlooked.

The *President Harrison*, too, deserves to be remembered. As the inaugurator of the round-the-world service that came to represent the zenith of the modern peacetime American merchant marine, as the 502 that best personified the Shipping Board's goal of a ship that could serve her country in peace and war, and as a ship that was too tough to die at her own hands and had to be destroyed by the nation that built her, she has earned a niche as a near-legend in American maritime history. She was, indeed, unsurpassed in playing so many roles with such competence and class--truly a ship for all seasons and for all seas.

NOTES

Chapter 1

The early history of the U.S. Shipping Board appears in the book by Smith and Betters. Descriptions of the transports of World War I have been fashioned from a number of sources, including Emmons and Kludas. Isherwood's comments on the appearance of the transports are found in articles in *Sea Breezes*.

The contingency plans of American President Lines to use additional presidential ship names are mentioned in a company statement in 1963 entitled, "American President Lines--President Liners." The history of the Dollar Line and APL is from John Niven's definitive book, The *American President Lines and its Forebears, 1848-1984*, and from an article by W. J. Granberg.

The shipping magazine reporting the 1926 grounding of the *Harrison* was the *Shipping Register*. The correct location of the grounding, Bonham Island, was provided by Emmons, and confirmed by Valdemar Nielsen who was aboard the ship at the time.

The historical background leading up to World War II is from Morison and Bergamini.

Chapter 2

Much of the information in this chapter is from John Hallinan of San Francisco, a purser's clerk on the Harrison. Details concerning the crew are from the ship's official crew list, furnished by Hallinan. Crewing practices of American President Lines and other steamship companies are described in Niven.

Sailing cards for American President Lines were supplied by *Pacific Shipper* magazine. The Naval Reserve status of the *Harrison* and similar ships is explained in Lovette. The war zone bonuses are described in the various court cases immediately following the war, and are summarized in *Agnew* vs. *American President Lines* in *American Maritime Cases*.

Chapter 3

The background on the military situation in the Far East is from Morison's *History of United States Naval Operations in World War II*, Volume 3, *The Rising Sun in the Pacific*. The details of the selection of the *Harrison* for the Shanghai mission and the trip itself are from Captain Pierson's post-war report to the company. The role of the *President Madison* was explained by Captain Nielsen.

Descriptions of the Marines in the International Settlement draw upon books by Millett and Williams, as well as an unsigned photo essay in Naval Institute *Proceedings*. The farewell party for the Marines in Shanghai was described by two attendees: Captain Valdemar Nielsen and Captain Louis Duncan, USMC (Ret.), who was an enlisted man in the 4th Marines. The song with the reference to Shanghai is the "Marines Song," words by Al Dubin, music by Harry Warren, published by Remick Music Company in 1937.

Details of the departure of the Marines came from *New York Times* accounts, the official Marine Corps history of the war, and eyewitnesses such as Captain Duncan and Carla Allan, a spectator to the parade. Colonel Howard's report on the loading problems is quoted in the official Marine Corps history.

Chapter 4

The major source of information on the voyage north to Chinwangtao and the capture of the ship is the narrative of Captain Pierson, put together shortly after the war. Recollections of individual crew members and the passenger agent are also utilized, some of which contradict each other and those of the captain.

The availability of other ships in November 1941 has been reconstructed from Army records, newspaper stories, and records of the San Francisco Marine Exchange. The location of Navy transports is from the *Dictionary of American Naval Fighting Ships* and from Fahey's *Ships and Aircraft of the U.S. Fleet*; the submarine situation is from Morison.

Preparations for the arrival of the *Harrison* in North China are described by White, Janus, and Foley. The story by the radio operator Madden was originally published in the 1971 yearbook of the Society of Wireless Pioneers, and was reprinted in the Santa Ana (CA) *Register*. The consideration given to the Chusan Archipelago as the site for an American naval base at the turn of the century is described by Hoyt.

Chapter 5

Most of the details of the salvage operation are from accounts of Captain Pierson, crewmembers Behrens, Treadway, and Hallinan, and passenger agent Wise. The series of articles in *Yomiuri Shinbun* was also useful.

The menu for the Christmas dinner was supplied by John Hallinan who also furnished a series of snapshots taken aboard the ship at Shaweishan Island from which it was possible to draw conclusions about the salvage work. The food and water situation on board was described by Behrens, Wise, and by the family of Third Mate Olsen.

Information on the other scuttled and salvaged ships is from an article by the senior author in the Monterey (CA) Peninsula *Herald*. Observations on salvage technique reflect the senior author's training as a Navy salvage and diving officer shortly after World War II.

Chapter 6

The capture of the *Wake* and the destruction of the *Peterel* are described in books by Reynolds, Oldham, and Wettern; these accounts have been amplified by the testimony of two *Peterel* survivors. The Sam Logan story appeared in *Colliers*; although generally accepted by the Navy, the story has some inexplicable aspects.

Events in North China are described in White and Janus, as well as in the official Marine Corps history of the war and in the *Yomiuri Shinbun* series. Accounts of the sinking of the *Malama* and *Vincent* are from Moore's book on World War II merchant shipping casualties.

Major sources on life in the Woosung and Kiangwan camps include books by White and Janus; other sources include books by Reynolds, Devereux, Cunningham, and Oldham, plus eyewitness accounts by Foley, Pollard, Thatcher, Newton, and Dupuich.

Escape attempts from the Shanghai camps are described by C.D. Smith and Cunningham; escapes involving 4th Marines are cited in Kerr's book on prisoners in the Pacific War. Survival rates for various prisoners are extrapolated from data in Kerr.

Chapter 7

Colonel Ashurst's citation was provided by the U.S. Marine Corps Historical Center. The concept of *bushido* is explained in Bergamini's book, *Japan's Imperial Conspiracy*.

The U.S. Naval Group, China, is described in Miles' book, *A Different Kind of War*. The role of the radioman from the *Peterel* who remained at large is the focus of Wettern's book. Captain Schact's article in Naval Institute *Proceedings* is useful in understanding the issues of the *Code of Conduct*.

Chapter 8

Eyewitness accounts provide most of the information about the crew in Shanghai and in the internment camps. Particularly helpful are those of John Hallinan, Gilbert Monreal, Henry Behrens, and Howard Allred who kept a valuable scrapbook. Also useful are the manuscript of George Laycock, John Potter's recollections in his wife's book, Arch Carey's book, and the deposition and recollections of Henry F. Kay. The escapes from Shanghai are described in Laycock in the case of the banker, and in a personal recollection by Sam Logan from the crew of the *Wake*.

Repatriations are discussed by Kerr. Details of life in the internment camps are confirmed by several civilian residents of Chapei and Yu Yuen Road, and by Ballard's autobiographical novel about Lungwha. Deaths of prisoners are reported in Moore's book; the sparse details of these deaths are supplied by crewmembers.

Chapter 9

The American flag remaining on the hull of the *Harrison* is reported by Cunningham, and confirmed in a picture appearing in a Shanghai newspaper. The additional sinkings of unnamed Japanese vessels by American submarines are reported in Roscoe's book on submarine activity in World War II. The details of the sinking of the *Kachidoki Maru* are from the Blair and Blair book, *Return from the River Kwai*, and from the action report of the USS *Pampanito* and its subsequent endorsements. Accounts of other sinkings of prisoner ships are largely from Kerr. Estimates of the number of prisoners killed in transit are from Spector.

Chapter 10

The location of prison camps as one of the surrender terms, is explained by Kerr. The experiences of liberation and repatriation are from personal recollections of crewmembers. The red tape encountered by the crew of the *Malama* is described by the rescuer, Captain William Aguilar of the *Cape Meares*. The legal actions by the crew to regain the war bonus are contained in voluminous records at the National Archives in San Bruno, California.

The transfer of American President Lines back to private ownership is detailed in Niven. The events of 1988 affecting the crew are described in various newspaper accounts. Dr. Foley's observation about reparations to Japanese Americans came in a personal interview.

Chapter 11

Primary sources for this chapter are books by Janus and Shapiro, articles by Dr. Foley and others, and the newspaper series from *Yomiuri Shinbun*. The report of Janus' legal difficulties appeared in the *New York Times*. John Carey's theory on the disappearance of Peking Man came in a recent interview.

The reviewer of the Taschdjian book for the *New York Times* was Caroline Seebohm.

Chapter 12

The reference to the Marines burning their belongings at Olongapo is attributable to Louis Duncan of the 4th Regiment. The War Claims Act is codified in Title 50, *U.S. Code*; relevant paragraphs are 2004 for internees, 2005 for prisoners of war, and 2015 for merchant seamen.

BIBLIOGRAPHY

PRIMARY SOURCES

Unpublished Materials

James M. Agnew Jr., et al vs. *American President Lines*, and related cases. Record Group 276, Boxes 11943-11946, National Archives, San Bruno, CA.

Gerald X. Beeman, "Peking Man, A Summary and Analysis," 20-page manuscript, n.d.

Henry Behrens, "SS *President Harrison*, The Story of a Ship and Her Crew," 21-page manuscript, 1946.

Crew List, SS President Harrison, voyage 55.

Marilyn J. Grover, "The Legacy of the Treaty Port System," 23-page research paper, University of California, Davis, 1984.

Admiral Thomas C. Hart, USN, "Narrative of Events, Asiatic Fleet, Leading Up to War and from 8 December 1941 to 15 February 1942."

-- Sailing Orders for *President Harrison* and *President Madison*, and related correspondence. November 18 and 27, 1941.

George W. Laycock, "Prisoner of Cathay," 152-page manuscript, n.d.

W. G. MacDonald, "American President Lines--President Liners," 1-page statement on ship naming policies, 1963.

Ervin R. O'Neale, 3-page statement of internment-related health problems, March 24, 1986.

USS *Pampanito*, Action Report, September 28, 1944.

-- Report of War Patrol Three, September 28, 1944.

Orel A. Pierson, 2-page statement on the fate of the ship, October 24, 1945.

-- 7-page report to Operating Manager of American President Lines on loss of *President Harrison*, n.d.

E. S. Wise, "Twice a Prisoner of Japan," 3-page manuscript, n.d.

Commander John B. Woolley, RN, Report to Commander-in-Chief, Portsmouth, September 18, 1945.

Newspapers and News Magazines

Assembly Times, Chapei Civil Assembly Center, various issues, 1943.

Freedom, Japanese propaganda publication, n.d.

London *Times*, October 5, 1945.

New York Times, November 28, December 10, 1941; December 5, 1943; November 3, 11, 1944; September 18, 1945; February 4, 1952; May 11, 1980; February 26, May 30, 1981; January 21, 1988.

Pacific Shipper, September 29, October 13, 20, 27, 1941.

San Francisco *Chronicle*, November 7, 1926; November 28, December 8-10, 1941; March 26, 1988.

Shanghai *China Press*, November 9, 11, 1941.

Shanghai *Evening Post and Mercury*, American edition, various issues, 1943.

Shanghai *North China Daily News*, November 26-28, December 3-7, 1941.

Shipping Register, November 13, 20, 1926; June 14, July 19, November 1, 1941

Shipping Review, October 11, 1941.

West Coast Sailor, October 26, 1945.

Interviews and Correspondence

CREW OF THE HARRISON
>James M. Agnew Jr.
>Howard Allred
>Henry W. Behrens
>John Hallinan
>Paul Hugli
>Gilbert Monreal
>Captain Orel A. Pierson
>Alfred Rye
>Jasper Treadway
>Albert Triger

EARLIER STATEMENTS OF DECEASED CREWMEMBERS
>Joaquin "Mike" Barassa
>Roy Madden

FAMILY AND FRIENDS OF DECEASED CREWMEMBERS
Robert W. Harbut
Captain Eugene Harrower
Richard W. Kennedy
Bonnie Olsen McDonnell
Mrs. Sydney Olsen
Captain Archibald Simenstad
Captain Michael Simenstad

PRISONERS AT WOOSUNG/KIANGWAN CAMPS
Leon Dupuich
William T. Foley, M.D.
Colonel George Newton, USMC (Ret.)
Captain Gordon Pollard
Frank Thatcher Jr.
Colonel John A. White, USMC (Ret.)

MEMBERS OF THE 4TH MARINE REGIMENT
Captain Louis Duncan, USMC (Ret.)

CREW OF THE WAKE
Sam Logan
William Loughner

CREW OF THE PETEREL AND SURVIVING RELATIVES
Mrs. Jack Honeywill
Jim Mariner
J. B. Polkinghorn
C. M. Williams

INTERNEES AND/OR RESIDENTS OF SHANGHAI
Carla Dannver Allan
J. G. Ballard
Margaret W. Clarke
Ruth Roth Clifford
Sophie Fox
Patrick S. Gibons
Pauline Schinazi Witts

EMPLOYEES OF AMERICAN PRESIDENT LINES
Colette Carey

John Carey
Captain John Chiles
Henry F. Kay
W. G. MacDonald
Captain Valdemar Nielsen
E. S. Wise
George Zellensky

HISTORIANS
Dr. William Braisted
Charles Dana Gibson
Dwight B. Messimer
Captain Arthur R. Moore
Dr. John Niven
Commander Peter Oldham, RNZNR
Rear Admiral Kemp Tolley, USN (Ret.)
Desmond Wettern

OTHER INDIVIDUALS
Captain William Aguilar
Russell Booth
Lieutenant Commander Frank C. Brown, USN
Pat Hall
Chief Warrant Officer Cecil S. King, USN (Ret.)
William Kooiman

GOVERNMENT ENTITIES
American Embassy, Tokyo
British Consulate General, San Francisco
Imperial War Museum, London
Library, Marine Corps Air Station, El Toro, CA
Ministry of Defence, London
National Archives, Washington, DC; San Bruno, CA
National Maritime Museum, Greenwich, England
National Maritime Museum, San Francisco
Naval Historical Center, Washington, DC
Office of Information, U.S. Navy
Royal New Zealand Navy
U.S. Marine Corps Historical Center
U.S. State Department

OTHER ORGANIZATIONS OR FIRMS
　　　Allen Knight Maritime Museum
　　　American Defenders of Bataan and Corregidor
　　　American Ex-Prisoners of War
　　　American Museum of Natural History, New York
　　　Burns, Philp & Co., LTD, Sydney
　　　Cornell University Medical College
　　　Lillick, McHose & Charles, San Francisco
　　　Marine Digest Magazine
　　　Marine Society, London
　　　International Order of Masters, Mates and Pilots
　　　Naval Reserve Association
　　　National Maritime Museum Association, San Francisco
　　　New Zealand Military Historical Society
　　　Puget Sound Maritime Historical Society
　　　The Retired Officer Magazine
　　　San Francisco Marine Exchange
　　　Sea Breezes Magazine
　　　Society of Wireless Pioneers
　　　Steamship Historical Society of America
　　　Television Station KQED, San Francisco
　　　U.S. Naval Institute, Photographic & Oral History
　　　　　Sections

SECONDARY SOURCES

Books

All About Shanghai and Environs, A Standard Guide Book.
　　　Taipei: Chen Wan Publishing Co., 1973 (reprint of pre-
　　　WWII edition).
American Maritime Cases. Baltimore: American Maritime Cases,
　　　Inc., 1947 and 1949.
Ballard, J. G., *Empire of the Sun.* New York: Simon and
　　　Schuster, 1984.
Barber, Noel, *The Fall of Shanghai.* New York: Coward,
　　　McCann, & Geohegan, 1977.
Bergamini, David, *Japan's Imperial Conspiracy.* New York:
　　　Pocket Books, 1972.
Blair, Clay, Jr., Silent Victory, *The U.S. Submarine War Against*

Japan. Philadelphia and New York: J. B. Lippincott Co., 1975.

Blair, Clay, Jr. and Blair, Joan, *Return from the River Kwai*. New York: Simon and Schuster, 1979.

Booker, Edna Lee, and Potter, John S., *Flight from China*. New York: The Macmillan Co., 1945.

Brice, Martin H., *The Royal Navy and the Sino-Japanese Incident, 1937-41*. London: Ian Allen, 1973.

British and Foreign Merchant Vessels Lost or Damaged by Enemy Action During Second World War. London: Naval Staff (Trade Division), Admiralty, 1945.

Brown, F. C., Lella, John E. and Sullivan, Roger J., *The 4th Marines and Soochow Creek*. Bennington, VT: International Graphics Corporation, 1980.

Carey, Arch, *The War Years at Shanghai, 1941-45-48*. New York: Vantage Press, 1967.

Condit, Kenneth W., and Turnbladn, Edwin T., *Hold High the Torch, A History of the 4th Marines*. Washington, DC: Historical Branch, Headquarters, U.S. Marine Corps, 1960.

Conway's All the World's Fighting Ships, 1922-1946. London: Conway Maritime Press, 1980.

Cunningham, W. S., with Sims, Lydel, *Wake Island Command*. Boston: Little Brown, 1961.

Devereux, James P. S., *The Story of Wake Island*. New York: J. B. Lippincott, 1947.

Dictionary of American Naval Fighting Ships. Washington, DC: Naval Historical Center, 1959-81.

Dollar, Robert, *Memoirs of Robert Dollar*, Volume 3. San Francisco: Robert Dollar, 1925.

Emmons, Fredrick, *American Passengers Ships, The Ocean Liners, 1873-1983*. Newark, DE: University of Delaware Press, 1985.

Erdman, Robert P., *Reserve Officers' Manual, U.S. Navy*. Washington, DC: U.S. Government Printing Office, 1923.

Evans, William R., *Soochow and the 4th Marines*. Rogue River, OR: Atwood Publishing Co., 1987.

Fahey, James C., *The Ships and Aircraft of the United States Fleet, Two Ocean Fleet Edition*. New York: Ships and Aircraft Publishing, 1941.

Frank, Benis, M. and Shaw, Henry I., Jr., *History of U.S. Marine*

Corps Operations in World War II, Volume V, *Victory and Occupation*. Washington, DC: Historical Branch, U.S. Marine Corps, n.d.

Griffin, W. E. B., *The Corps, Semper Fi*. New York: Berkley Publishing, 1986.

Haines, Gregory, *Gunboats on the Great River*. London: MacDonald and Janes, 1976.

Hough, Frank O., et al, *History of U.S. Marine Corps Operations in World War II*, Volume I, *Pearl Harbor to Guadacanal*. Washington, DC: Historical Branch, U.S. Marine Corps, n.d.

Hoyt, Edwin P., *The Lonely Ships, The Life and Death of the U.S. Asiatic Fleet*. New York: David McKay Company, 1976.

Janus, Christopher G., with Brasher, William, *The Search for Peking Man*. New York: Macmillan Publishing Co., 1975.

Japanese Naval and Merchant Shipping Losses During World War II by All Causes. Washington, DC: The Joint Army-Navy Assessment Committee, 1947.

Japanese Naval Vessels of World War II, as seen by U.S. Naval Intelligence. Annapolis, MD: Naval Institute Press, 1987.

Kerr, E. Bartlett, *Surrender and Survival, The Experiences of American POWs in the Pacific 1941-1945*. New York: William Morrow & Co., 1985.

Kludas, Arnold, *Great Passenger Ships of the World*, Volume 2, *1913-23*. Cambridge, England: Patrick Stephens, 1976.

Kreh, William R., *Citizen Sailors, The U.S. Naval Reserve in War and Peace*. New York: David McKay Company, 1969.

Lloyd's Register of Shipping. London: Lloyd's Register of Shipping; annual, various years.

Lovette, Leland P., *Naval Customs, Traditions, and Usage*. Annapolis, MD: U.S. Naval Institute, 1939.

Lucas, Mary, and Lucas, Ellen, *Teilhard*. Garden City, NY: Doubleday & Co., 1977.

MacDonald, W. G., *History of American President Lines Vessels*. Oakland, CA: American President Lines, looseleaf notebook, n.d.

The H. W. McCurdy Marine History of the Northwest. Seattle: Superior Publishing Co., 1966.

185

Merchant Vessels of the United States. Washington, DC: Various
federal agencies; annual, various years.

Metcalf, Clyde H., *A History of the United States Marine Corps*.
New York: Putnam & Sons, 1939.

Miles, Milton E., *A Different Kind of War*. New York: Doubleday & Co., 1947.

Millett, Allan R., *Semper Fidelis, The History of the United States
Marine Corps*. New York: Macmillan Publishing Co.,
1980.

Moore, Arthur, *A Careless Word . . . A Needless Sinking*. Kings
Point, NY: American Merchant Marine Museum, 1988.

Morison, Samuel E., *History of the United States Naval Operations in World War II*, Volume 3, *The Rising Sun in
the Pacific*. Boston: Little, Brown & Co., 1953.

Moskin, J. Robert, *The U.S. Marine Corps Story*. New York:
McGraw Hill Book Company, 1977.

Niven, John, *The American President Lines and Its Forebears,
1848-1984*. Newark, DE: University of Delaware Press,
1987.

Oldham, Peter, *Lieutenant Stephen Polkinghorn, DSC, RNR*.
Aukland: New Zealand Military Historical Society, 1984.

Register of Ships Owned by the United States Shipping Board.
Washington, DC: U.S. Shipping Board, 1921.

Reisenberg, Felix, *Sea War, The Story of the U.S. Merchant
Marine in World War II*. New York: Rinehart & Co.,
1956.

Report of the Future Development of the Shanghai Harbour
(report to the Whangpoo Conservancy Board). Shanghai: 1918.

Review of Pre-War Merchant Shipping in Far Eastern Waters.
Chungking, China: William Hunt & Co., Federal Inc.,
USA, 1944.

Reynolds, Quentin, *Officially Dead, The Story of Commander
C. D. Smith*. New York: Random House, 1945.

Roscoe, Theodore, *United States Submarine Operations in World
War II*. Annapolis, MD: Naval Institute Press, 1949.

Sailing Directions for the Coast of China. Washington, DC:
Government Printing Office, 1943.

Sailing Directions for the Coasts of Korea and China. Washington, DC: Defense Mapping Agency, 1987.

Shapiro, Henry L., *Peking Man*. New York: Simon and Schuster,

1974.

Smith, Darrell Hevenor, and Betters, Paul V., *The United States Shipping Board, Its History, Activities and Organization*. Washington, DC: The Brookings Institute, 1931.

Spector, Ronald H., *Eagle Against the Sun*. New York: The Free Press, 1985.

Stanley, Roy M., II, *Prelude to Pearl Harbor*. New York: Charles Scribner's Sons, 1982.

Talbot-Booth, E. C., editor, *Merchant Ships, 1943*. London: Macmillan & Co., 1944.

Tolley, Kemp, *Yangtze Patrol, The U.S. Navy in China*. Annapolis, MD: Naval Institute Press, 1971.

Wainwright, Jonathan, and Considine, Robert, editor, *General Wainwight's Story*. Garden City, NY: Doubleday & Co., 1946.

The War Against Japan. London: Her Majesty's Stationery Office, 1957.

Watts, Anthony J., *Japanese Warships of World War II*. Garden City, NY: Doubleday & Co., 1967.

Wettern, Desmond, *The Lonely Battle*. London: W. H. Allen, 1960.

White, John A., *The U.S. Marines in North China*. Millbrae, CA: John A. White, 1974.

Williams Robert Hugh, *The Old Corps, A Portrait of the U.S. Marine Corps Between the Wars*. Annapolis, MD: Naval Institute Press, 1982.

Willmot, H. P., *Empires in the Balance, Japanese and Allied Pacific Strategies to April 1942*. Annapolis, MD: Naval Institute Press, 1982.

Winslow, W. G., *The Fleet the Gods Forgot: The U.S. Asiatic Fleet in World War II*. Annapolis, MD: Naval Institute Press, 1982.

Magazine Articles

Adair, Charles, "As I Recall--End of Peace in the Philippines," Naval Institute *Proceedings*, August 1985.

Booth, Russell, "USS *Pampanito*, The Third War Patrol," *Sea Letter*, Summer 1985.

-- "USS Pampanito, The Last Three War Patrols," *Sea*

Letter, Spring 1987.

Brown, F. C., "The Disappearance of 'Peking Man'--A Tale of Old China," *Military Collectors' Journal*, July-August 1984.

-- "The Mystery of Peking *Man*," *U.S. Navy Medicine*, January-February 1985.

Caraccio, David, "Vet Tells Story of War He Barely Survived," Clear Lake (CA) *Observer*, August 26, 1988.

Coffin, Roberta Tong, "Shanghai at War," *The China Gunboatman*, March 1989.

Cox, Janet, "Whatever Happened to Peking Man?" *Harvard Magazine*, September 1974.

Foley, William T., M.D., "A Small Contribution to the Mystery of Peking Man," Cornell University Medical College *Alumnus Quarterly*, Winter 1971-72.

Gordon, John, IV, "The Navy's Infantry at Bataan," Naval Institute *Proceedings*, March 1985.

Granberg, W. J. "'Dollar Debacle' to Dollars and Sense," *Ships and the Sea*, Fall 1985.

Grover, David H., "The Turncoat Transport: *President Harrison*," *Sea Classics*, March 1988.

-- "U.S. Ships Sailing Under Enemy Colors," Monterey (CA) Peninsula *Herald*, September 22, 1985.

Isherwood, J. H., "Steamers of the Past: U.S. Liner *'President Roosevelt'* of 1922," *Sea Breezes*, undated clipping.

-- "The U.S. Mail Liner *'Blue Hen State'* of 1921," *Sea Breezes*, February 1976.

"Japs Lie About U.S. Prisoners," *Life*, September, 14, 1942.

Jensen, Owen E., "Escape from Shanghai, Fourth Marines Leave China Just Before War," *Leatherneck*, January 1943.

Lederer, William J., "The American Navy Is in the Middle of China," Naval Institute *Proceedings*, August 1942.

Logan, Samuel, as told to Dorsey, George, "Japan Hits Below the Belt," *Colliers*, July 18, 1942.

Lowman, David, D., "The Treasure of the *Awa Maru*," Naval Institute *Proceedings*, August 1982.

Madden, Roy W. "Sparks". "High Treason in World War II? Another Version," Santa Ana (CA) *Register*, December 12, 1971.

Magruder, John H. III, "Last Passenger Ship Out of the Orient," *Saturday Evening Post*, July 25, 1942.

Miles, Milton E., "U.S. Naval Group, China," Naval Institute

Proceedings, July 1946.

Mydans, Shelly S., "Letter from Mormugao: Repatriated from Japanese Internments Camps," *Life*, November 29, 1943.

Porter, W. B., "Gunboat Saga," Naval Institute *Proceedings*, April 1944.

Schact, Kenneth G., "Reflections on the Code of Conduct," Naval Institute *Proceedings*, April 1982.

"Shanghai Duty 1937-1938, How Bittersweet it Was," Naval Institute *Proceedings*, November 1974.

Smith, Columbus D., "Report on China," Naval Institute *Proceedings*, September 1950.

Toda, Takashi, "The Mystery of Peking Man," Tokyo *Yomiuri Shinbun*, June 30-July 5, July 7-12, July 14-19, July 21-24, 1980.

Tolley, Kemp, "Divided We Fell," Naval Institute *Proceedings*, October 1966.

Van Peenen, H. J., "Touchstone from Zentsuji," *The Retired Officer*, December 1986.

"Where is Peking Man?" *Science*, March 27, 1959.

INDEX

196

Powell, J. B., 103
President Buchanan, 9
President Coolidge, 7, 42
President Cleveland, 170
President Fillmore, 7
President Grant (502), 42, 44, 113, 124, 170
President Grant (535), 30
President Harrison, early history, 1-10; voyage to Manila, 11-22; voyage to Shanghai, 23-40; voyage to Chinwangtao, 41-45, 47-54; grounding and capture, 54-60; salvage, 61-69; as Japanese ship, 119-125; sinking by *Pampanito*, 125-133; possible role in Peking Man affair, 161-163; tribute to, 171-172.
President Hayes, 16
President Hoover, 7-8
President Johnson, 7
President Madison, 26-34, 37-39, 137, 142, 145, 162
President Pierce, 42, 80, 170
President Polk (502), 16, 28
President Polk (C3), 17
President Taft, 17, 42, 57
President Taylor, 23, 42, 170
President Van Buren, 28
Prince of Wales, 59
prisoner of war medal, 148-149
Pueblo incident, 93
Puerto Princesa prison camp, 90
Puget Sound Maritime Historical Society, 121

Queenfish, USS, 130, 159

Rainbow 5 War Plan, 23-24, 166-167
Rakuyo Maru, 125-130
Raspe, Herman G., 88
Ray, Claude, M. D., 115
Refuge, USS, 39, 137
reparations for relocated Japanese-Americans, 149-150
repatriation, efforts for Marines, 81-82; in 1942 for diplomats, 105; in 1943 for civilians, 113
Republic, USS, 42
Ridgely, Maj. Reginald H., Jr., 34
Robert L. Barnes, USS, 62

ONE RIVER,
MANY WELLS